My Job SUCKS And I Can't Take it Anymore!

HELP!

The Real-Life Job Survival Guide

John L. White

First Edition

Everlove and Bohannon Publishing
Wesley Chapel, FL

My Job SUCKS And I Can't Take it Anymore!
HELP!
The Real-Life Job Survival Guide
by John L. White

Published by:
Everlove and Bohannon Publishing
Post Office Box 7411
Wesley Chapel, FL 33544-0107
everlovebohannon@aol.com

ISBN 13: 978-0-9740687-9-4
ISBN 10: 0-9740687-9-9
First Printing 2007
Printed in the United States of America

Publisher's Cataloging-in-Publication
(Provided by Quality Books, Inc.)

White, John L., 1957-
My job sucks and I can't take it anymore! : help! : the real life job survival guide / John L. White. -- 1st ed.
    p. cm.
    Includes index.
    LCCN 2005910216
    ISBN-13: 978-0-9740687-9-4
    ISBN-10: 0-9740687-9-9

    1. Work--Psychological aspects. 2. Success--Psychological aspects. 3. Job satisfaction.
I. Title.

BF481.W45 2007   158.1
                           QBI07-600018

Dedication

This book is dedicated to Larry Kim.

Acknowledgments

I would like to thank my brother, James A. White, Ph.D., Denise Janes, Joe and Mary Berling, and Sean Cavanagh for their valuable input on an early draft of the manuscript.

Many thanks to Lois P. Frankel, Ph.D., for taking the time to review selected chapters from the manuscript and provide valuable feedback.

Thanks for the creative and honest counsel of my Financial Advisor, Mark Gray, MBA.

All my love to my beautiful, intelligent wife, Keri. Her keen sense of humor and wit help keep me on my toes. She also never lets me forget that even though this is now my second published book, I still need to take the garbage out every week.

To my funny, sweet, smart, and lovely teenage daughters, Mary and Kathleen. You have made my life full, rich, and wonderful.

Contents

PART THREE
Life as a Cube Dweller

PART FOUR
What to do When Your Job Disappears

PART FIVE
Achieving Nirvana (Or How I Learned To Make My Job Not Suck So Much)

IMPORTANT- DISCLAIMER

Introduction

Are you stressed out at work? Do you hate your job?

Does your job just basically **SUCK**?

If you have ever answered yes to any of these questions, then this is the book for you.

If you're like me, you weren't born with a silver spoon, you aren't a trust fund baby, and you haven't yet saved up enough money to be financially independent. You've got bills to pay and responsibilities to keep, but it's getting harder and harder to get out of bed every morning to go to work. I know, I've been there before and I may be there at some time again in the future.

I've been in the work force for 30 years now (God, how depressing is *that*?). I've been a white-collar worker, a blue-collar worker, and when I was young, a McJob worker. I've been stressed out, dumped on, pissed off, and laid off.

There have been many times I've been so mad that I just wanted to quit and walk away (and when I was very young, I did that a few times). That's a viable option when you don't have any responsibilities, but now it really isn't something I can do anymore. I have a mortgage to pay and people who depend on me, so I've had to find a way to survive through all the frustration, all the stupidity, and all the heartache of the modern workplace.

Over the years I've developed some strategies, tips, and ways of thinking that have made work more tolerable and less frustrating than it used to be. Since work is somewhat universal, and human nature is too, I'm betting that a lot of the strategies and tips I've developed will work for you too.

I'm at a place now in my current job where I'm fairly content. I don't love my work, but I don't hate it either. I'm a professional and I do a good job. I would like to stay for several more years, maybe even retire. The problem is, I don't know if I'll even be allowed to retire. Because of globalization concerns (hey dude, where's my job?) and the fact that I'm now an older, highly paid "resource", I sometimes feel like I've got a big red bulls eye on my chest.

I want to stay, but will my company let me? Will I be one of the unfortunate "chosen ones" in the next round of layoffs? Accordingly, I also cover different strategies and tips you can use to try and stay one step ahead of the layoff executioner.

Throughout this book I have provided real life anecdotes from the various jobs I've had, followed by the lessons I have learned and the strategies I've developed. *All of the anecdotes are true.* Some are pretty funny, and some are pretty sad. They are arranged in chronological order, beginning with my first working experiences.

The book is broken down into five sections:

1. The McJob Years
2. Blue Collar Blues
3. Life as a Cube Dweller
4. What to do When Your Job Disappears
5. Achieving Nirvana (Or How I Learned To Make My Job Not Suck So Much)

The bulk of the advice offered from the early work experiences fall under the "lessons learned" category. I've included everything, the good, the bad and the ugly. No punches are pulled. At the end of each section, there will be a summary of the lessons and tips.

In section 4, I cover different strategies that can help protect you from ever having to say: "Welcome to Crapmart" or having to train your overseas job replacement.

In section 5, "Achieving Nirvana", I discuss specific philosophies and mindsets for surviving in the workplace.

What you'll notice is that depending on where you are in life and the type of job you have, the lessons, options and strategies may differ. So, it doesn't matter whether you're 17 or 65, there's probably something in this book you can relate to and benefit from.

A goodly portion of the later sections of the book are devoted to survival in the corporate workplace. As anyone who has worked in a large corporation can testify, it can be exceedingly frustrating. Corporations have their own perverse set of rules that are frequently at odds with any rules of common sense that would apply in a sane world. Recognizing and understanding those counter-intuitive rules can help you survive in the "upside down" world of corporate America.

If you work for a large company or corporation, I think you'll appreciate that I don't engage in any "spin doctoring" in my descriptions of life in a large company. What is depicted here is not your Father's workplace of thirty years ago. There is no sugar coating of the truth. Quite frequently, our preconceived notions of how the workplace should function can clash with the reality we encounter on a day-to-day basis. Learning to recognize a situation for what it really is can help to alleviate some of the disappointment you feel when reality doesn't meet your expectations. The upside of facing that sometimes difficult reality is that you can develop a mindset which allows you to deal with the inequities of the workplace with less stress, less frustration, and potentially less hours spent on the job.

One other thing you may have noticed, I haven't used the word career to describe my job. There's a critical distinction between those two words and it's one of the most important strategies contained in this book.

PART ONE

The McJob Years

The Red Death

You always remember your first job…

You're probably in high school, still living at home with Mom and Dad, so you're not making money to pay no stinkin' bills! You're in the enviable position of making money for the sole purpose of gratifying some fleeting desire. As soon as the cash from your miniscule paycheck hits your pocket, you can blow it on clothes, music, going to the movies, whatever you want.

My first job was working as a busboy in a seafood restaurant. A guy I knew at school who worked there said he could get me the job. I wasn't even old enough to drive (I was fifteen).

This was my first exposure to the "Food Industry". It was an eye opening experience, I had no idea how disgusting a restaurant could be. The first day I was on the job, I saw one of the cooks drop a hamburger patty on the greasy tile floor, pick it up, and throw it back on the grill.

There were two primary duties a busboy performed: clearing dirty tables and dumping the garbage. With regard to rules, there is only one I still remember: there was an in door and an out door to the kitchen. I made that mistake only once. During my first week on the job, I headed toward the kitchen with a bus pan full of dirty dishes and chose the wrong door. When a hustling waitress came out, the door flew open, I got knocked on my ass, and the bus pan went flying.

With regard to bussing the tables, you either did it by yourself, or if it was a large table, you cleared it with one of the other busboys. There was this one guy who was kind of the "top dog" of the bussing crew. The first time I cleared a table with him, he picked up one of those little white cups containing cocktail sauce and smeared it down my forearm while demonically uttering "*The red DEATH*". It kind of surprised me, so I didn't really respond to it. He was much larger than me and I still felt insecure about my whole place in the bus boy pecking order. About a week later, he did the same thing. I think I said something to him, but once again, I didn't do anything about it. However, the more I thought about it, the angrier I got. I promised myself that if he did it to me again, I would do something about it. My fragile young ego could only take so much.

The third time he did it, I picked up one of those little plastic coffee creamers, pointed it at his face, and squeezed. It EXPLODED all over his shirt, his face, and his hair. He had little white droplets in his eyebrows and one hanging off his nose. He was so pissed off, I thought he would kick my ass... but he didn't... he also never did the "Red Death" to me again.

Tip: *Never let anyone push you around on the job.*

The other delightful duty that we performed was dumping the garbage. There was this huge garbage can in the kitchen that held coffee grounds, fish crud, disgusting refuse of every variety. By the end of the evening, it would be full of crap like that. It was so big and heavy that it took two guys to dump it. You would position yourselves on either side of the container, grab the handle with one hand, lift it up high enough to grab the bottom with your other hand, then hoist it up so you could pour it into the dumpster.

There was this one wimpy little busboy that had a "bad back". Whenever I was teamed up with him, I would almost rupture myself because I was doing ninety percent of the lifting. I asked him a few times if he could help out more, but he never did. One night when I was dog tired and pissed off at him, I decided I'd had enough of his wimpy routine.

When we got the container over our heads, I took control (which wasn't hard because he barely had a hold on it) and dumped some of it on top of him. As he wiped the fish heads and coffee grounds off himself, he whined to me: "Why did you do that?". I told him he had to start putting some effort into it, that I was tired of killing myself lifting that crap with no help from him. After that, amazingly, his bad back got better and the container got much lighter. From then on, I never had to strain myself as much when I was lifting it with him.

Tip: *Never let anyone take advantage of you on the job.*

The other type of people I had to deal with were the waitresses. In general, they treated the bus boys like they were the lowest form of life on the planet. Unfortunately, there was a reason for this. One of the busboys had been stealing tips from them.

One night when we were very busy, a waitress accused me of stealing her tip. Either one of the other busboys grabbed it off the table before I got there, or the customer stiffed her. This woman was about the same age as my mother, so I was put in the uncomfortable position of having to defend myself against someone who felt like she was in a position of authority just because she was older than I was. I protested my innocence but she didn't believe me. She even told some of the other waitresses that I had stolen her tip money. From then on, I was saddled with the undeserved reputation among the waitresses of being a thief. I was perfectly innocent, but there was nothing I could do about it.

Lesson: *Sometimes you get screwed, and there's nothing you can do about it. You just have to let it go.*

I do have to mention the one good thing about this job that seemed like a tremendous perk to me at the time. We got to eat for FREE! To a fifteen year old, that's like winning the lottery. With the exception of expensive dishes like steak and lobster, we could have anything off the menu. I always wondered if my food had been dropped on the floor or spit on, but hey, free food is free food...

I eventually got sick of the job and quit. I think the two main things that made me leave were the way I smelled at the end of the night because of the fish crud garbage (I would have to shower off as soon as I got home) and the constant tension between the busboys and the waitresses.

So, the tip to be learned here is the old standby, that time honored teenage worker's tradition that you can always exercise when you have no bills to pay and no responsibilities. Good ol' Mom and Dad are still footing the bill for everything (after all, isn't that why God put them on this earth?).

YOU CAN JUST QUIT!

Tip: *If your job sucks bad enough, you can always quit. Remember that this tip comes with a condition: You can't be in a position where you're responsible for anyone or anything.*

Beware of Jobs With The Word "boy" In The Title

After a "hiatus" of about a year, I took my second High School job. Ironically, it also had the word boy in the title. I should have learned from my previous experience to be suspicious of any job title that included the word boy, but hey, once again, I was driven by the want for money. I now had my regular driver's license and was starting to take girls out on car dates (hallelujah!). I needed some cash to support this newly discovered, exciting lifestyle. Sometimes my brother would even let me borrow his red Pontiac Firebird with the 8-track stereo for dates, but then again, that's another story…

The job I took was in a grocery store as a bag boy. A bag boy's duties consisted of bagging groceries, collecting carts in the parking lot (my favorite "I'm working, but not really working" activity. I would have spent all day in the parking lot if they had let me), unloading trucks, pricing items (this was back before digital scanners, every single item had to have a price tag), cleaning up the occasional jar of mayonnaise that some cart riding spastic kid had snatched off the shelf and dropped, cleaning the bathrooms (this is when I learned that the woman's bathroom is far more disgusting than the men's room), and mopping the floors (by hand) at the end of the evening.

One Saturday, toward the end of a very busy day, I was in the stock room talking with one of the bag boys when Dan, another bag boy (my friend who initially told me about the job) walked up with three ice cream bars. Being naive, I didn't even think about how he got the ice cream. We were still eating them when up walked the assistant manager. With my mouth still full of Eskimo pie, he started lecturing me about stealing the store's stock. About this time, the reality of the situation began to dawn on me. I also noticed that the other guys had already ditched their ice cream somewhere and were looking at me with wide "keep your mouth shut" eyes. I decided to take the bullet and stay silent on the whole deal. The lecture ended with something like, "If you get caught doing that again, we'll be forced to take action".

Lesson: *Sometimes you just have to keep your mouth shut*

The thing I hated most about the job was mopping the floors at the end of the night. If it was Friday or Saturday, you had assistance from the other bag boys. But on weeknights, at the end of the evening, there would only be one bag boy working, so you had to mop the entire store by yourself. First, you had to sweep the whole store. Then you went and got this big fifty-five gallon drum that contained the old mopping water from the night before. It was mounted on wheels, so you would have to roll it outside to the parking lot and dump it into the storm drain (this thing felt like it weighed a ton). Then you would drag it back inside, pour in some cleaning solution and fill it up with water. Then you were ready to start mopping.

Being your typical, lazy teenager, one night I got the exceptionally bright idea that I could just skip the whole "clean mopping water" routine and mop the store with the water from the night before. I was about three quarters of the way through when up came the assistant manager with a distressed look on his face. He said: *"**What** are you mopping with?"*, I said: "Why?", he replied: *"The   floor is all streaked!"*. At that point, I fessed up to using the old water from the night before. He actually took it pretty well and helped me go back and mop the part of the floor that I had screwed up. I didn't realize until I got older that this guy probably had a family to get home to and had to wait every night until the bonehead bag boy had finished mopping the store before he could go home.

Lesson: *There are some rules that have no purpose, therefore, they can and should be broken. There are other rules that are there for a good reason and you should always follow them. The important part is knowing the difference.*

I eventually quit this job after not quite a year. When I walked away, I promised myself that I would never work in a restaurant or grocery store again. So far, I've been able to keep that promise…

Bring On The "Real World"

After I graduated from High School, I attended Community College while working part time as a teacher's aide. I had actually started while I was still in High School through a new program called the "Credit Bank", meaning you could bank College credit hours before graduating from High School.

I was still living at home with my parents and saving most of the money I earned. During that time I had many concerns about my future and did quite a bit of thinking about what I was going to do. I knew I had reached a point where I was supposed to be making decisions about my "future direction". But to be honest, like any typical teenager, I had no clue about what that might be. I really didn't know what I wanted to "do with my life".

About the only thing I did know was that I reached a point where I just didn't want to go to school any more. I'm not saying it was a wise decision, but it was what I felt like I had to do at that time. I wanted to get on with my life and it felt like I was just spinning my wheels at school. I wanted to experience the "real world".

Little did I know that the real world had some real hard lessons in store for me.

The McJob Years Summary:

Tip: *Never let anyone push you around on the job.*

Tip: *Never let anyone take advantage of you on the job.*

Lesson: *Sometimes you get screwed and there's nothing you can do about it. You just have to let it go.*

Tip: *If the job sucks bad enough, you can always quit. Remember that this tip comes with a condition: You can't be in a position where you're responsible for anything or anyone.*

Lesson: *Sometimes you just have to keep your mouth shut*

Lesson: *There are some rules that have no purpose, therefore, they can and should be broken. There are other rules that are there for a good reason and you should always follow them. The important part is knowing the difference.*

PART TWO

Blue Collar Blues

The Toxic Job

I decided that I wanted to move out of my parent's house. I called up my older brother and asked him if I could share his apartment (he had moved out of the house a few years before and had a decent job working at the gas company). I offered to pay part of the rent and utilities. Being the good brother that he is, he said yes, so I packed up my stuff and moved out.

After I got settled into the apartment, I began interviewing for different jobs. One in particular that I didn't take really stands out in my mind.

The job was at a company that built yachts. The particular position they offered me was the person who ran a machine called the "chopper". The chopper was a hand held tool that chopped up fiberglass into tiny particles while simultaneously spraying it on the hull of the boat. The boat they were working on when this was demonstrated to me was situated in front of an open warehouse door. The mid morning sun streaming in through the open door illuminated an over spray of a million little particles of fiberglass floating in the air. Even though most of the employees were wearing masks, my first thought was that it might not be too healthy working in an environment like that day in and day out. The guy that interviewed me looked stunned when I turned down this "great job". The money was good, but I figured it wasn't worth my health.

Tip: *Think twice before taking any job that looks like it could cause long-term health problems.*

Dark Warehouses, Bad Dogs, and Big Cockroaches

After a few more interviewing dead ends, I eventually took a job as a delivery driver for a sign supply company. We delivered all the parts and materials that companies use to make signs.

Early in the morning, we would get our routing sheets and load our trucks. We delivered many different types of items: plexiglass, transformers, wire, glass tubing, etc.

Every night before we left work, they let the owner's (I'll refer to him as Mr. Silverman) dog loose in the warehouse to prevent anyone from breaking in and stealing stuff. This dog was vicious. One of the employees who had been there for a long time was the only guy other than the owner who could get close to him without getting bit. Every morning, he would get the dog and put him into another room so we could go locate the parts we needed to load into our trucks.

I really hated this part of the job because the dog would crap on the warehouse floor during the night. As you were loading stuff, you had to be careful that you didn't step into a dog shit land mine.

In addition, the warehouse was loaded with cockroaches. Mind you, this is in Florida where the roaches are so big you can put a saddle on them. But here's the really gross part: there would usually be a swarm of roaches feasting on the piles of dog crap when you first entered the warehouse.

The warehouse was also very poorly lit. Sometimes you would have to climb a ladder in some dark corner and dig around on a shelf for the part you wanted. There was more than one time when a cockroach skittered across my hand while pulling some item out.

All of this grossness was somewhat made up for by all the "windshield" time you got. For the uninitiated, windshield time is driving time. To a young man, driving is still fun, so getting paid to drive doesn't really feel like work.

After I had been there a few weeks, Silverman called me into his office. By the look on his face, I could tell he wasn't very happy. He asked me if I had been letting any of the customers look at other customer's delivery information.

Initially, I said no, but when I thought about it, I realized that the delivery sheets for all the customers were kept on the same clipboard. At some of the stops, the customer would want to hold the clipboard to look at the order information so they could verify what they were receiving. When I was busy unloading the truck, some of them must have been rifling through the other customer's orders. I didn't realize that each customer's order information was considered confidential, competitive information. The thought had never even crossed my mind. With a pained look on his face, Silverman explained all this to me. From that point on, I made sure I only had the order for the customer I was unloading on the clipboard.

Lesson: *Don't forget that the owner is in business to make money. If you remember to protect his or her interests, it can make your work life easier.*

The company employed two drivers, myself and a black man that I'll refer to as Carl. I would guess that Carl was about thirty. He was married and had a couple of kids. He was a hard worker and a real nice guy.

One day, when he was out sick, I handled his delivery route. While making a delivery at the largest account we had, this little middle-aged guy came up to me and asked me where the "boogie" was. I had never heard this term before. I said, "what?". He said: "Where's the boogie, you know, the black guy". I told him he had the day off. However, the more I thought about it, what he said really bothered me because I liked Carl. I really didn't know what to do about it.

The next day I decided to tell Carl what that guy said. He was really pissed off because he had always acted friendly toward him, like he was his buddy. Well, I guess Carl said something to him the next time he made a delivery, because a few days later, Silverman called Carl into his office to have a discussion with him.

Silverman told him that he shouldn't take what that guy said personally. He went on to explain that because he was Jewish, he could understand being discriminated against. He went on to tell him that he was in business to make money and that money was colorblind. I'm not sure what else he said to Carl, but it seemed like it worked because he wasn't so angry anymore. It's funny, I've thought about that situation a few times since then. I had good intentions, but I know that the information upset Carl. I'm also pretty sure that it didn't change the other guy's opinion of minorities either. In addition, it forced Silverman to deal with a situation that he really couldn't control. This was by far the largest account he had, and there was no way he wanted to lose that customer. Moreover, I think it made Silverman start to view me as just being a pain in the ass, trouble-making employee. I know I did the right thing but sometimes I think that all it did was to cause unnecessary grief.

I'm not sure if there is a lesson or a tip that can be derived here, but I thought I would relate the story because it's an example of the kind of difficult situation you can be put into in the workplace.

After working there a few months, I came in one day and found out that we had no deliveries to make. Silverman assigned us to clean up a large pile of junk that was near the loading dock. It was full of broken parts, scrap metal, and old pallets.

While cleaning up the pile, I stepped on a piece of an old pallet with a nail sticking out of it. Luckily, it didn't puncture my foot too deeply. Trying to be conscientious, but being totally naive about the fears a small business owner might have about an on the job accident, I went and told Silverman.

I said that I thought it might need to be checked out just to make sure that it wouldn't become a problem. Well, he came unglued... He started swearing at me for wearing sneakers instead of work boots. I proceeded to tell him that he couldn't talk to me like that. He said he could talk to me any way he damn well pleased. So I said: "I don't need this crap,

I quit!'". We both stormed into the office. He had the accountant make out my last check and that was the end of that job.

Looking back, I now realize that this guy probably just viewed me as being a pain in the ass kid who caused problems. However, there was no excuse for his behavior that day. Since then, I've never encountered any manager or owner who was as verbally abusive as that.

Lesson: *Don't take verbal abuse from anyone.*

"You Ain't No Po-lice"

My next job turned out to be the shortest job I ever had. I didn't even last a day.

After reading an ad in the paper, I applied for a job as a security guard. I thought this sounded pretty good. I had visions of guarding construction sites or maybe condominiums, some gravy assignment like that.

I went down to their office, filled out all the paper work and they hired me. Then they told me what my assignment was:

Crowd Control at the welfare office.

I wasn't quite sure what "Crowd Control" entailed and why it would need to be done at the welfare office, but I had a gut feeling that it didn't sound so good. I expressed some concerns but they reassured me that it wasn't a big deal. Plus, I wouldn't be by myself. I would be assigned to work with "Old Joe". They said he was a good guy who would show me the ropes and take me under his wing... So with some misgivings, and against my gut feeling, I went ahead and reported to my first day of work.

I showed up bright and early at the welfare office and met "Old Joe". He was an overweight, middle-aged man. We attempted to have a conversation, but I could barely understand what he said. With the assistance of some hand gestures, I figured out that he wanted me to go outside with the crowd while he stayed inside.

The outside duty consisted of letting in only a limited number of people at a time into the welfare office. Being a quick study, I surmised that this was where the "crowd control" part came in. He also either said or perhaps I assumed (albeit, wrongly) that we would trade off after a while.

So, summoning up all my intestinal fortitude, I went outside to literally, face the crowd.

There were at least seventy people waiting in line and none of them looked very happy. And here I was, stuck with the onerous task of telling some of them that they could go inside while telling others that they had to wait for their turn.

Well, it didn't take very long before this situation went south. One woman came up to me, opened her eyes real wide, flared her nostrils and said: "You ain't no po-lice, you ain't even got's no gun.". Then I heard another one behind her say: "You one skinny white boy, what you doin here?"

At that point, I began to wonder the same thing myself.

When I looked back inside I could see Old Joe hard at work, drinking coffee and eating a donut while flirting with one of the clerks. Behind me, I heard: "How he goin stop us from goin in der?" "He cain't…"

At that point, I decided to *ease* myself back inside to tell Old Joe that I needed some help. He grunted something like "unh unh, you go on back out". It became obvious that he had no intention of going outside. As a matter of fact, I was encroaching on his prime flirting time. He'd probably been working on this woman for weeks and here I was, cramping his style. So I turned around, walked back outside and kept on walking. I didn't stop until I reached my car, then I drove away.

Lesson: *If a job doesn't feel right, it probably isn't, so be honest with yourself and don't accept it. You'll be doing both yourself and your potential employer a favor.*

Timing Is Everything

Fortunately, before I moved out of my parent's house to begin my "real life", I had saved up about $2,500 dollars. This was back in 1976, so that was a lot more money than it is today. As it turns out, I wound up using it to help support myself between jobs and to supplement my income while I was working jobs that didn't pay so well.

Unfortunately, all good things must come to an end and so did my money. I had about $500 dollars left, with no good job prospects in sight. I also had no intentions of moving back home.

Summoning up all my courage, I went down to the Air Force recruiting office and started inquiring about a "Career" with the Air Force. Even though they put pressure on me, I didn't sign anything. I decided I would take a little while to think about it before I made a permanent decision.

About a week later, I received what turned out to be a life altering phone call. It was a friend of the family who worked as a manager with the local power company. He told me that I could have an interview within the next few days. I had actually interviewed for a job with them over a year before.

While I had him on the phone I asked him why they hadn't hired me back then. He said they were afraid I was going to go to College and wouldn't be interested in keeping the job that long. I went to the second interview and they made me an offer. Very happily, I accepted.

It was an interesting matter of timing, if he had called about a week later, it would have been too late, I probably would have already enlisted. But as it turned out, I was now on a course that led to what I would consider my first good job.

Climbing Poles and Digging Holes

Four dollars and two cents an hour. I still remember exactly what the salary was when I started working at the power company. I think that was about twice the amount minimum wage paid back then. I couldn't imagine what I was going to do with all that money. It was even enough to get my own apartment. The job was located about thirty miles north of my brother's place and was pretty close to my parent's house, so I moved back in with them for a few weeks, just long enough to find my own apartment.

When I look back on that job, it's almost like viewing another person's life. It's so very different from what I do today to make a living. To begin with, it was a very macho atmosphere. Almost all the guys I worked with were big and burly. You never worked alone, you always worked with someone, and you were always outside. At times, the work was very physically demanding, in fact, it was the hardest work I've ever done. It was also potentially dangerous, but I thought it was the type of danger that could be controlled, depending on how careful you were.

I showed up about an hour early for my first day at work. Even so, there was another guy already there. He was one of the Senior Lineman. Later on, I found out that they were called "Journeyman" Lineman. In the Lineman pecking order, that was the top of the food chain. A Journeyman was essentially a working foreman. He usually had one or two other lesser-qualified Lineman that he supervised.

Mr. Early bird offered me some coffee. I thanked him, but said I didn't drink it (I hadn't developed my morning coffee addiction yet). He looked at me like I was some sort of wimp, then went back to reading the morning paper. I had only been on the job for about five minutes but I already felt like I had failed some vital test of my manhood.

There were various types of crews or "trucks" you could be assigned to. There were "overhead" crews and "underground" crews. Overhead is a reference to the power lines and poles that you see every day along the roadside. Within the overhead classification, there were "bucket" trucks and "digger" trucks. The bucket truck is the one that lifts someone up into the air so they can work on the power lines. The digger truck has a large corkscrew device called an auger that's used to dig holes to set the poles into.

The underground trucks have big reels of insulated wire on them. They usually tow a trailer that contains a ditching machine or backhoe. Those crews bury and work on the underground power cables that you never see. The only physical evidence is the big green boxes (transformers) that sit on the ground.

I was initially assigned to work on a "service" truck. It was a small bucket truck. We handled any power outage calls that might come in during the day. We also connected and reconnected the power at people's houses. Sometimes we would hang a transformer on a pole and run the service wire to a house. Periodically, when there was no work of that type to be done, we would be assigned for the day to work with a line crew to help build new power lines. It was just about the best truck to be assigned to, because the work wasn't too physically taxing, and you got loads of "windshield" time.

Even so, at the end of the day, I would come home exhausted. During my first few months there, I would sometimes go home and fall asleep on the couch for a couple of hours, wake up at about 7 or 8 pm, get something to eat, then go back to sleep.

Initially, my nemesis was a crimping device that we used called the "Anderson" tool. It was a hydraulic tool used to crimp metal connectors on wire. The hydraulic "power" was provided by the person operating the tool. It had 2 handles that extended from the crimping head that you would have to open and close using your arm strength. As you "pumped" this tool, little metal protrusions in the head of it would crimp down on the connector, fastening it to the wire. I could barely operate it with my scrawny little eighteen-year-old spaghetti arms. It took all the strength I had just to finish the crimp. Sometimes I would resort to resting the tool against my thigh while I was using it. It became kind of a joke among the other linemen that the Anderson tool was "kicking my ass".

This was also the first job where I became aware of a distinct culture and language. I've already mentioned that the environment was macho. In addition, there was a strong dose of redneck thrown in for good measure. Many of the other Linemen spoke with a distinctly southern twang. Face to face, I didn't have any trouble understanding them, however, when they spoke on the radio, it was another story. In particular, working on the service truck involved plenty of radio communication. For the first few months, I simply could not understand a lot of the conversations on the company radio. However, after a while it became second nature and I could understand everything (I'm still not sure whether that was a good thing or a bad thing).

The company's main office was located in a rural southern town that was about twenty five miles from the branch office I worked out of. Entering that little town was like stepping back in time about fifty years. The first few times I was there, I attempted to strike up a conversation with one of the employees. Usually, the only responses I would get were very abrupt one or two word answers. The entire atmosphere can probably be summed up with one phrase that was never uttered but could be felt down in your gut:

"You ain't from around here are ya boy?".

A large part of the redneck "culture" involved hunting, fishing, and guns. There were endless discussions involving the relative merits of different types of hunting, various fishing spots, what fishing lures were the best ones to use, who caught the biggest bass that weekend, etc. Many of the guys drove trucks that had gun racks in the rear window. Some even had handguns under the seat or in the glove box.

Initially, I was definitely viewed as an outsider in this environment. Not only was I skinny and weak of arm, but I also didn't hunt, fish, or own a firearm. This was tantamount to being considered a homosexual (and at the power company, that's about the worst thing you could be). However, I expressed an interest in learning about these "manly arts" and over time I was at least tolerated, if not considered one of the group.

Tip: *Every work environment has a culture. Your work life will be much easier if you can fit into that culture.*

Over time, I began to fit in, and eventually learned to like the job. It was very different than anything I had ever done before, so it was kind of a challenge to see how good I could be at it.

One of the reasons I liked working there were the constant practical jokes. Of course, there were rules against "horse play". All of the supervisors gave it lip service, but they knew what was going on. They had all been linemen at one time and had done their share of screwing around on the job.

An extreme example of this all started innocently enough one morning as I was putting new batteries in our flashlights. I was just getting ready to throw the old batteries in the dumpster when my foreman (we'll call him Don) walked up with a wild-eyed look on his face. He said:

"*Whoa*, wait a minute, what are you doing? Don't throw those away! Don't you *know* what that is?".

I paused for a moment, then glanced down at the batteries in my hands.

"OK... looks like dead batteries to me, but obviously, it's something else".

With an evil grin, he replied: "That's... *ammunition*".

I wasn't exactly sure what he had in mind, but it sounded like it might not only be fun, but also had the potential to be destructive, so I put them back on the truck and away we went.

A few hours later, we were in a very wooded, rural part of the County. To be honest, I can't remember who decided what the target of choice was, but we settled on the perennial favorite of all testosterone driven adolescents (the obvious exception to this being that I was about twenty years old and Don was about thirty, but hey, you're only as young as you feel… and on that day, I think we were both about thirteen).

I can still feel the wind in my hair and the grin on my face as I leaned out the passenger window of the truck, eyes wide open, stinging from the wind.

I cocked my arm back, D cell in hand, took aim at that first mailbox and let it rip…

BLAM!

A direct hit! At about fifty miles an hour!

MUUUAHAHAHAHA!

Even today, it makes me laugh just thinking about it. Hearing the explosion of the battery hitting that mailbox was a thrill in itself.

After a while, we switched off. I drove so Don could be the passenger side gunner. I think we scored about a seventy five percent target delivery success rate that day. And the best part is that we were getting *paid* while doing it.

What a **GREAT** job!

Before you get the wrong idea, I need to point out that the previous example of wonton vandalism was extremely rare (it must have been a full moon and the tides were high that day, or something…). The horseplay was normally directed at our fellow employees, it didn't normally involve abuse or destruction of property. We were both totally out of our minds that day. But… it was a heck of a lot of fun…

When we built a new power line, one guy would be up in the bucket, working on the pole, the other guy would be on the ground. After the guy working on the pole was finished, he would lower the bucket back down on the truck, get out of it, then get in the cab so we could drive to the next pole. However, quite frequently, instead of getting out, he would stay in the bucket while the other guy drove to the next pole. It was quicker and easier, it was also a direct violation of company safety policies.

One day, when I was the guy in the bucket, Don got behind the wheel to ostensibly drive us to the next pole. However, as we approached the next pole, instead of applying the brake, he tromped down on the gas pedal and wrenched the steering wheel violently to the right. We jumped the gutter and headed into a vacant lot that contained quite a few large oak trees. He had decided it was time for a little "off road" rally.

With each rut and bump we hit, the bucket would jump up a few feet, then slam back down. This was exacerbated by a "catapaulting" effect from the boom that the bucket is attached to. With every jolt, my feet would come flying off the bottom of the bucket. I took a white knuckled grip on the front edge and held on as tight as I could to keep from being bounced out. For reasons only understood by testosterone driven young men, after the first lap around the lot, I started to like it a little bit, so I let out a: "**YEEEE HAAAA!!!**" at the top of my lungs.

After zooming around the lot a few times at breakneck speed, Don obviously got bored and decided to up the ante.

The next thing I knew, we were headed for the low hanging branches of an oak tree. I ducked down real low in the bucket to keep my head from being taken off. Small branches scraped across my knuckles and the top of the bucket. The truck was littered with twigs and leaves when we emerged from the other side of the tree.

I guess its just part of my personality, but I have to admit that it was a heck of a lot of fun. I also didn't forget it, and as soon as I got my chance, I took him on an even wilder ride one day.

Tip: *As much as possible, try to have fun at work. It will make a good job better and sometimes make a crappy job tolerable. (However, you probably shouldn't engage in activities that are as potentially dangerous or destructive as the previous examples...)*

Be Careful What You Wish For

After I had been on the job for a while, I decided that I wanted to go for the "Brass Ring" and become a Journeyman Lineman. I'm using the term decided somewhat loosely, because to tell you the truth, I don't actually remember sitting down and weighing all the pros and cons about whether or not it was worth it to be a Journeyman. I guess some of the decision was due to the increase in pay, however, looking back, the additional money wasn't all that significant. Perhaps more of it was driven by the "common knowledge" that you always want to advance as far as possible in your job.

In general, our society (and every corporation I've worked for) teaches that advancement, promotion, and additional responsibility are always good things. I'm now old enough and experienced enough to know that the next step up in a job is not necessarily the best move to make.

Tip: *Always weigh the pros and cons of accepting a job "promotion", particularly if it will involve managing people in any fashion. Don't be influenced by what you "ought" to do or be flattered into taking a position that involves more work and responsibility if it's not what you really want.*

It took a minimum of five years experience to become a Journeyman lineman. You also had to take a written exam and pass an oral review board. The oral review process consisted of being thrust in front of a panel of eight or nine members of the senior staff (engineers, the safety director, etc.). Each of them took turns asking questions about how you would approach certain situations or solve a given problem.

Having made my decision that I wanted to advance to this next level, I studied pretty diligently for the exam. I even went out on the weekend with my wife, driving around, looking at which substations all the main circuits were fed from because I heard that was one of the questions they might ask.

After I passed the written exam, I was scheduled to go before the review board. I remember being pretty nervous before it started, but once I got in front of everyone and began to answer questions, my nervousness totally disappeared. It became obvious to me that they were *trying* to make me nervous, that's what this game was all about.

Whenever they brought up a hypothetical situation, only part of the information you needed would be provided, then they would pressure you to respond. They were attempting to rattle the candidates so they would answer incorrectly based on incomplete information.

Instead of immediately answering, I would ask them questions until I had enough information to answer correctly. At one point, they even balked at providing me with an answer. One of them said:

"Just tell us what you would do, *make a decision*".

I refused, with the explanation that if I was in the field, diagnosing the problem, I would gather whatever information I needed before I made my decision. I guess that response was acceptable, because they gave me more information.

Responding in that fashion accomplished a couple of different things. Not only did it provide me with the information I needed, it also allowed me the benefit of changing the pace of the process. Instead of being in a totally passive role, it put me on more of an equal footing with the folks who were firing all the questions at me.

There was only one time that I made an obvious error. It involved an imaginary scenario where you were sent to a substation that had a circuit breaker which exploded and was on fire. The task you were given was to run through the steps of how you would bypass the bad breaker. At one point, I gave the wrong answer, but then immediately caught myself. My answer came out something like this:

"First I would do X, then I would do Y, then I would do Z… no… **shit**, that's not right".

No sooner had I said shit than one of the managers said with a big laugh: "I guess that was a oops, eh?". This, of course, evoked great laughter from everyone in the room.

However, as I said, that was the only obvious error I made, and apparently, the strategy I used worked, because I found out later that I passed with a unanimous vote.

There are a few tips that can be derived from this:

Tip: *Don't be intimidated by someone's title or position, if you let yourself be intimidated, it will automatically put you at a disadvantage.*

Tip: *Don't be afraid to take control of a situation if you need to.*

Tip: *If you need more information to make a correct decision, don't be afraid to ask. Be persistent if you have to.*

Another one of the guys who went in front of the review board at the same time I did just barely received a passing vote. This was very ironic and almost tragic because he was a better lineman than me. I was later told that he was exceptionally nervous during the entire review process (behavior he never exhibited in the field). The flawed assumption the review board made was that the verbal pressure of being in front of a review board was equivalent to the pressure of working on a real problem out in the field.

Lesson: *Sometimes there is a difference between doing your job well and management's criteria for judging how well you perform in that job. In many cases, the metrics you are evaluated by may have nothing to do with how proficient you are at performing your job.*

At that point, I was what was referred to as "Journeyman Qualified". That meant I could do all the work a Journeyman did (Journeyman also performed potentially dangerous live wire work that other linemen were not certified to do), but I did not have my own truck and crew. I would have to wait until they needed to put another crew on the road before my pay would be increased.

The Standoff

After not quite a year, the branch manager of my office decided that he needed to add another crew. At the time, there were three of us who were Journeyman qualified. They decided to offer the position to me because I had a few more months of experience than the other two guys. However, I soon found out that there was a catch.

My supervisor at the time was decent enough to pull me aside and give me a heads up about what was going to happen (or maybe he was just trying to prep me for the screwing I was about to receive, either way, I was glad he did it). He told me in confidence that the branch manager decided to offer me the job, but not officially promote me to Journeyman. The alleged reason was he did not know how long they would need to keep that crew on the road, so he didn't want to promote me before it was absolutely necessary.

I instantly knew the official reason was pure bullshit. It was a poorly kept secret that the branch manager (let's call him Dick) thought that lineman were overpaid for what they did.

I'm sure this was partly due to his work experience or lack thereof. He had never been a lineman. His entire career had consisted of office work, therefore, he had no feeling for what the job really entailed. On top of that, he was a mean spirited individual. He actually said the following to my wife and me one time: "You know, when a young guy starts working here and he buys a new car, we know we have him for a little while. But then, when he gets married and buys a house, we know we have him for life."

That is an amazing statement for someone to make. However, once you get past the arrogance of it, you'll find that there's some truth contained within it.

Many of the guys who worked there were what we called "job scared", meaning that they felt like they needed the job so bad that they would endure any kind of crap that management threw at them. They suffered in silence because they felt like they were trapped.

It didn't take a genius to realize that Dick's real motivation for not promoting me was to make himself look good. He could put another crew on the road, get more work done, and keep his payroll down because they wouldn't have to pay me the additional money a Journeyman made. He could then report to the main office that he got more work done for less money.

I guess my supervisor could tell by the look on my face that I was livid. He tried to reason with me:

"John, just take the job, you'll eventually get promoted, but don't make the wrong decision… take the job."

I thanked him for giving me the advance notice and told him I would think about it.

At that point, I was essentially put into a no win situation. I knew that I could not accept the position under those terms. I also knew that if I balked at the offer, Dick would never forget about it. He was a singularly vindictive individual. I knew he would do his best to get even with me in some way.

The good part (if there was one), was knowing this information beforehand. It gave me some time to think about all the possible reasons they might throw at me in an attempt to get me to accept the position. I knew exactly what I needed to say to them when the time came.

Tip: *Inside information can be extremely valuable. Always keep in touch with the office grapevine or any potential information sources you may have.*

When this great "opportunity" was presented to me, Dick didn't even do it himself. He had the operations superintendent talk to me. He wasn't a bad guy, but it was obvious that Dick had told him what to say.

After he laid this golden opportunity at my feet, I told him that if they wanted me to take on the additional responsibility, they would have to promote me. Accordingly, he said they weren't sure how long they would need to keep the crew on the road and they didn't want to have an employee earning Journeyman pay who wasn't leading a crew. I said:

"Fair enough, if that happens, then reduce my pay back down to where it was before."

He responded with: "You're not being fair!" (I have to admit, this response did surprise me a little bit... *I wasn't being fair?*). So I told him:

"You're the one who's not being fair. I did all the studying, spent my own time preparing, passed all the tests, and now you're telling me I can have the job, but you don't want to pay me for it. So, you tell me, who's not being fair?"

Seeing how he couldn't really argue the point, he put the ultimate threat on the table: "If you don't take the job, we'll offer it to one of the other guys. If one of them accepts, you'll be put at the bottom of the list!" I said: "Fine, go right ahead".

He told me he would have to think about it and get back to me, which really meant "I have to go talk to Dick and have him tell me what to do".

The really unfortunate part of all this was now the entire situation was put under a microscope. As soon as I walked out of the office, it seemed like everyone knew exactly what had happened. All the employees were now watching with interest, anxiously waiting to see what would happen with this standoff. It was me against Dick. Blue-collar worker against the manager everyone hated.

The problem was, even if Dick backed down, who knew what his planned retaliation would be in the future? I had no doubt that he would eventually find some way to win the war even if he lost the battle.

One thought immediately came to mind. Every year for the last few years running, he had fired some poor unfortunate schmuck right before Christmas, just to make a point that he could do whatever he wanted (we were not unionized). We had even begun to engage in grim "gallows humor" speculation each Fall about who would be the "Christmas Child" that year.

However, as I expected, Dick eventually came to his senses. I think he realized that I was not going to back down. He probably also figured out that I was prepared to go to the main office with the information about the situation I was being put into. A few days later, they offered me the truck and the crew with a promotion to Journeyman.

Once the excitement of the promotion began to wear off, the reality of having two guys reporting to me began to settle in. To begin with, both of them were older than I was and I think they resented that a little bit. Also, neither of them were what you would consider a "Self Starter". We would pull up on a job site and instead of getting out of the truck and going to work, they would just sit there. They knew what had to be done (both of them had actually worked there longer than I had) but they would wait until I said, "OK guys, let's go to work…" They also did everything possible to avoid having to perform manual labor.

Our truck's primary function was to run the underground power cable from a transformer up to the side of a house and connect it to the meter box. We had a trenching machine that was used to dig the ditch for the cable. However, you always had to hand dig around the transformer using a shovel and also a few feet out from the house (it was safer and it also reduced the potential of damaging something).

Their propensity for laziness manifested itself in a particularly ridiculous fashion one day. I was unloading some material from the truck while they began to work on installing the cable to a house. I looked up just in time to see them back the trencher up and place the digging chain into the ground right next to the house (this probably would have saved them a whopping three to four feet of hand digging). As soon as the trencher was a few inches in the ground, it snatched the copper wire that ran from the meter box down to a ground rod. This started a bizarre chain reaction that not only pulled the copper wire off the side of the house, it pulled the meter box off too, but it didn't stop there... it also pulled all the pipe off the side of the house that went up into the attic. Watching this happen from a distance was like viewing a bad cartoon.

I had to go find the person who was in charge of construction at the subdivision and tell him what had happened. Fortunately, he gave me a break. Instead of billing the power company for fixing it (which would have caused me to be interrogated in grueling detail about what had happened), he said they would just take care of it.

From that point on, I gave my crew explicit instructions about everything. In addition, I always tried to keep an eye on them to make sure they weren't doing something that could cause damage. I began to wonder if the extra responsibility (I was responsible for *everything* these guys did) and aggravation was worth the few dollars an hour more that being a Journeyman paid.

Lesson: *Think twice before accepting any position where you have to manage people. If the money isn't a lot more than what you're currently making, it's probably not worth the additional headaches and aggravation.*

Sick Days? You Don't Need No Stinkin Sick Days!

After working as a Journeyman for not quite a year, Dick finally got his long awaited opportunity to display his vengeful nature.

The main office decided to produce a report that displayed any employee who currently had less than 40 hours of accumulated sick time (we received one week of sick time every year). These lists were then distributed to the branch managers.

Sensing a golden opportunity to browbeat employees, Dick decided that he would have meetings with each of the sick time "abusers" so he could stress the importance of banking your sick time instead of using it.

The meeting was held in his office. There were four people in attendance: Dick, the operations superintendent, my direct supervisor and myself. When I entered the room, Dick pointed to a chair and said: "Go ahead and sit on that hot seat, we've got it all wired up just for you…"

He started the "discussion" by reviewing the fact that I had less than forty hours of sick time banked. I responded by telling him that I had never abused my sick time. Every time I called in sick, I was really sick. As a matter of fact, I was dedicated enough to come into work after I had all four wisdom teeth pulled out. My supervisor had to send me home because I didn't look so good, that's how dedicated I was to the job.

Dick said: "Nobody here is saying you abused your sick time. What we're saying here is that we don't want people calling in sick... There are a hundred people out there who would love to take your job and those people would never call in sick. As a matter of fact, with you being a *newly made* Journeyman Lineman, your men depend on you to be here every day."

Then he held up another employee as the perfect example of the type of worker he wanted, this guy had never called in sick one day since he had been working there. Dick could not say enough great things about him. What made the situation even worse was that the guy he was using as an example would never become a Journeyman because he wasn't bright enough, he was very limited in what he could do (with good reason). This was Dick's example of the "perfect" employee.

When I went home that night, I felt sick to my stomach. In my heart, I knew that I had to quit, but just walking away wasn't so easy. It was decent money and good benefits.

Lesson: *Don't use your sick time. Some managers can and will hold it against you. Sure, most places will give lip service stating that it's better for a sick employee to stay home until they feel better and not spread it around the* *office. However, when it comes down to it, they want you to drag your sick self into work. It makes their utilization targets look better. Moreover, to some managers, it's a perverse litmus test of how "dedicated" you are.*

Worse than that, I had invested a lot of myself into the job. I had actually gotten to the point where I identified with being a Lineman. However, while I was mulling over this decision, something my old supervisor once said to me came to mind:

"Me? I'm not ever going to leave this job, I can't really do anything else... The bad part is that the company knows it too. They know they've got me and they screw me over every chance they get and there ain't a damn thing I can do about it.".

It's funny how something that a person might say in an offhand way can become important to someone else and they don't even realize it. I kept thinking about what he had said... I knew with every fiber of my being that I didn't ever want to be in that position.

Tip: *Don't ever get into the mindset where you think you're trapped in your job. It becomes a license for the company to abuse you. In addition, subconsciously you may begin to tolerate things you shouldn't.*

Fortunately, I'd had the foresight to be somewhat prepared for this moment. A few years earlier, I had told my wife that I knew I didn't want to stay at the power company forever. Being a lineman is a good job for a young man, but not for an old one. Also, my chances of becoming a supervisor before I turned fifty were slim to none. There were a ton of people with more seniority than I had. Plus, I still didn't quite fit the "Good Old Boy" mold that well. If you wanted to be a supervisor you usually had to go on a lot of hunting and fishing trips...

In light of this, we had started saving money every month. The goal was to save enough so we could live off of my wife's income supplemented by our savings for approximately two years (long enough for me to perhaps go back to school or get some training in another field.). We had enough for a little over one year saved up, so that made it a little easier to walk away.

I had actually wanted to stay on for a few more years to build up a bigger cash cushion, but it didn't turn out that way. I knew I had to leave.

I turned in my resignation the next day.

It's been twenty years now since I left that job.

However, sometimes in the afternoon while sitting at my desk, I daydream about zooming down rural streets, leaning out the passenger window of a truck, with the wind in my face, taking aim at some mailbox...

So This Is How The Other Half Works

After I left the power company, I had no real plan or idea about what I would do. Instead of going back to school, I spent the next two years working different jobs. One of those was working for a foreign-based company that had opened a branch office in Florida. They produced automated equipment for bakeries. My job was assembling and wiring electronic panels that were used to control the automated equipment. The main component of the control panel was a rudimentary computer known as a Programmable Logic Controller.

After I had assembled the control panel, I would wire it up in the warehouse so it could be programmed and tested. The construction of the building I worked in was designed such that the programmer's offices had glass walls that extended into the warehouse. While I was assembling the panels, I could look through those glass walls into their air conditioned offices and watch them "working". These were the primary work behaviors I observed: Sitting at a desk reading, sitting at a desk looking at a computer, sitting and talking to other programmers, and sitting and drinking coffee. From all outward appearances, this was obviously a job worthy of further investigation. I got my hands on some of the manuals used to program the controllers and took them home to read.

Fortunately, the company soon experienced a large growth spurt, which taxed the limits of the programming staff. Because they were so busy, there was no one available to program this one little system that was going to be installed in Mexico. I took a shot at it and found out that it wasn't that difficult.

I had also done some reading about "Jobs of the future". At that time, computer programmer was at the top of the list. Even better, published salary survey information I found indicated that it paid well. So, to my mind, this job seemed to be perfect. Top pay, high demand, job description: Read manuals and drink coffee all day. At long last, I had found my life's calling. My dream job awaited...

Now that I had a taste of the good life, I couldn't bear to perform manual labor any longer. I was "beyond that". I promptly quit my job and enrolled in Data Processing classes. I completed my Associate's degree in a little over one year. Feeling pumped from my success at school, armed with my little two year Data Processing degree, I was a proud thirty-year-old, ready to make the big bucks.

Blue Collar Blues Summary

Tip: *Think twice before taking any job that looks like it could cause long-term health problems.*

Lesson: *Don't forget that the owner is in business to make money. If you remember to protect his or her interests, it can make your work life easier.*

Lesson: *Don't take verbal abuse from anyone.*

Lesson: *If a job doesn't feel right, it probably isn't, so be honest with yourself and don't accept it. You'll be doing yourself and your potential employer a favor.*

Tip: *Every work environment has a culture. Your work life will be much easier if you can fit into that culture.*

Tip: *As much as possible, try to have fun at work. It will make a good job better and sometimes make a crappy job tolerable.*

Tip: *Always weigh the pros and cons of accepting a job "promotion", particularly if it will involve managing people in any fashion. Don't be influenced by what you "ought" to* *do or be flattered into taking a position that involves more work and responsibility if it's not what you really want to do.*

Tip: *Don't be intimidated by someone's title or position, if you let yourself be intimidated, it will automatically put you at a disadvantage.*

Tip: *Don't be afraid to take control of a situation if you need to.*

Tip: *If you need more information to make a correct decision, don't be afraid to ask. Be persistent if you have to.*

Lesson: *Sometimes there is a difference between doing your job well and management's criteria for judging how well you perform in that job. In many cases, the metrics you are evaluated by may have nothing to do with how proficient you are at performing your job.*

Tip: *Inside information can be extremely valuable. Always keep in touch with the office grapevine or any potential information sources you may have.*

Lesson: *Think twice before accepting any position where you have to manage people. If the money isn't a lot more than what you're currently making, it's probably not worth the additional headaches and aggravation.*

Lesson: *Don't use your sick time. Some managers can and will hold it against you. Sure, most places will give lip service stating that it's better for a sick employee to stay home until they feel better and not spread it around the office. However, when it comes down to it, they want you to drag your sick self into work. It makes their utilization* *targets look better. Moreover, to some managers, it's a perverse litmus test of how "dedicated" you are.*

Tip: *Don't ever get into the mindset where you think you're trapped in your job. It becomes a license for the company to abuse you. In addition, subconsciously you may begin to tolerate things you shouldn't.*

PART THREE

Life as a Cube Dweller

Paying My Dues

With great expectations, I started applying for programming jobs and waited for the offers to roll in. I waited, and waited, and then I waited some more... four months later, no job offers... Could it possibly be that I was competing against twenty-two year old graduates with Bachelor's degrees from prestigious universities? Or even worse... experienced, out of work programmers, looking for a job? With each passing day, my spirits dropped.

Just when things were really starting to look bleak, I received a break. At that time, my wife was working as a bookkeeper for a home-building partnership. During a discussion with one of the partners, she mentioned that her husband had a degree in Data Processing, but couldn't find a job. As luck would have it, the partner had a friend who managed programmers at a third party insurance administrator. He offered to give her my resume. The interviews went extremely well and I figured they would offer me a job. To say the least, I was excited. I imagined the salary would be good and the benefits would be excellent. Being rather naive about the realities of the corporate world, I had visions of a thirty-year career and a nice retirement.

However, when I got the job offer, reality set in: Title: Programmer Trainee, salary: a whopping $16,000 a year. *OUCH!* However, since I had no other prospects, I took the job to get the experience, with the hope that if I worked hard and distinguished myself, I would get promoted and finally get the salary I thought I deserved. As it turns out, I was half right.

Even though I was hired with the title of "Programmer Trainee", the first area I was assigned to work in was called the "Support Group". They performed an odd combination of duties. The primary responsibility was handling all the computer support calls that came into the Help Desk. In addition, they also produced one time or "ad hoc" reports for management using a programming language called "Nomad".

Looking back, I now realize that I was hired almost as an experiment. The company rarely hired programmers from community colleges. The last one they had hired before me turned out to be an abysmal failure, so they were reluctant to hire anyone who either didn't have experience or did not have a bachelor's degree. However, they agreed to hire me because they were taking a new "low risk" approach. Instead of bringing me directly into the programming group, I was brought into the support group with the understanding that I would only write Nomad programs, I wouldn't have to answer support calls. Over time, if I proved that I could actually write programs, they would transfer me into the programming area. In addition, it provided the company the benefit of getting a programmer at a dirt-cheap salary. For me, it provided the one thing that I needed most: experience.

The support group worked in what could only be referred to as a "barn-like" atmosphere. There were probably fifteen people in the group, and they all worked in one large room. This room was not partitioned in any way, the desks just sat out in the open. There were no cubicle walls to afford any sort of privacy.

As for me, I didn't even rate the luxury of a desk. In the very center of the room were two folding tables that were used to store manuals. They cleared off approximately one third of the space on top of one of these tables. This became my desk area. For storage space, instead of drawers or a filing cabinet, I was supplied with a cardboard box. Looking back, this was actually quite an appropriate beginning for my transition from Blue Collar to White Collar work

During my first week, I discovered that there were other unexpected benefits to working in the "barn". If any major system went down, this spawned the creation of a tiny little two-act play. Not only was I getting paid, but free entertainment was thrown in as an added bonus.

Act I consisted of a highly excited, loud declaration from the support person who had taken the initial call announcing this earth-shattering problem to the audience (the other support people who worked in the barn):

"CICS system XYZ is DOWN!".

Act II commenced with a self-important march up to a large white board that hung at the front of the Barn. Once there, the same person would write down the name of the failing system and what the problem was. I never did quite figure out why writing down the problem on the white board wasn't sufficient to satisfy the actual need. All that would have been required from the other support people was a glance in the direction of the white board to see if a problem already existed. Moreover, anyone tromping up to the white board was enough to get everyone's attention anyway. I guess simply walking up and writing something down didn't supply enough of a drama quotient for those involved.

However, the most unnerving aspect of working in the Barn didn't reveal itself until I had been there for about a week or so. I was sitting at my pseudo desk, diligently working on some fascinating coding task (at least it was fascinating to me back then), when I heard what I would have sworn was a barking seal:

"AR, AR, AR, AR, AR" !!!!

I whipped around to see that it was, in fact, one of the young women who worked in the Barn. Her excited laugh sounded exactly like a barking seal. It would have been more appropriate if she had actually been kneeling in her chair clapping her hands together instead of just sitting there.

Fortunately, my powers of concentration were more formidable then than they are today. In spite of the myriad distractions, I was able to focus on the programs I had to write. This was probably due to the fact that when I started working in data processing, I really enjoyed writing programs. There was a period of a few years during which I was totally focused on data processing.

I read everything I could get my hands on that would expand my body of knowledge. Even while eating my lunch, I would read and absorb dry technical manuals like some single focused, goal driven geek.

Panic In The Hallways

After working in this group for about four or five months, I had the experience of witnessing my first corporate layoff.

This corporation's philosophy toward layoffs required that the "chosen ones" had to immediately return to their desks to gather up their personal belongings. As soon as the pictures of the kids and the coffee mug were hastily dumped into a cardboard box, they were then promptly escorted out the front door. The official reason was for "security", but I thought it was an exceptionally cruel, humiliating way to treat someone who had given years of service to a company.

I made a vow to myself that if I was ever one of the "chosen", I would keep a clear head and stay calm at least until I got home. Little did I know that I would someday get the opportunity to put that strategy in action.

Tip: *If you ever get laid off (and the chances of that happening are pretty good these days), stay as claim as you can and ask for as much as you can (additional severance, etc). You may not get it, but it certainly doesn't hurt to ask.*

Tip: *If you're ever concerned about being "loyal" to the company, think again. Accept and embrace the reality that you are just a resource to them, nothing less, nothing more. They don't owe you anything. The flip side is that **you** don't owe them anything either. If you have trouble accepting that reality, never forget that if they need to get rid of you, you'll be gone the next day.*

During that first layoff, we received word about what was happening via the office grapevine in the middle of the morning. It continued throughout the entire day. It's hard to describe the demoralizing atmosphere of being in a building with everyone waiting and hoping they won't be called into an office to receive their corporate execution. You can almost smell the fear as it sweeps through the hallways.

I survived through the end of the day, but when I reported to work the next morning, my manager immediately called me into her office and asked me to close the door. This was something she had never asked me to do before... I figured that was it, I was a goner...

I guess she could tell by the look on my face that I thought I was getting whacked because she immediately reassured me I wasn't getting laid off. However, she informed me that I was being moved to another position called "Operations Analyst". Basically, they had created this position to keep me from being laid off because they were impressed with the work I had done during my short time there. It also didn't hurt that my salary was so small it wouldn't have amounted to a drop in the bucket anyway.

This new position consisted of helping to diagnose and fix any problems with the computer jobs that they ran every night. The good thing was that I didn't get called at night to fix them, it was normally stuff that was left over from the night before.

The woman I reported to was very nice and a pleasure to work for. One of her main tasks was to monitor the disk space for all the files that this business used (sort of like making sure you have enough space on your hard drive, except on a much larger scale). Every week, she would receive a report about the files. It contained information about how much disk space they were using and how much free space was available on each disk drive. The printed statistics for each file were fairly cryptic, but she knew how to interpret them to determine which files should be moved to another disk drive or needed to have space added to them to prevent a potential problem. This was a very tedious, boring, labor-intensive activity. She would have to read through these huge stacks of reports to compile a list of which files she needed to work on.

She knew that I had been hired as a programmer, so she asked me if I could write a program to automate some of this tedious work. I had her explain to me what pieces of information she looked at in the report that would indicate if there was a potential problem. I made a copy of the job that produced the paper report and had it send the output to a disk file instead of paper. Once that was done, I wrote a program that read the file so it could examine the information automatically.

The program contained logic that would perform all the same evaluations that she did manually to locate the potential problem files. When it found one of those files, it spit out the information to a report. The end result was a listing containing only the files that were a potential problem. This one program saved her many hours of work every month.

As an example of what a first class person she was (and is), she told her manager about what I had done, knowing full well that an accomplishment like that would help get me moved into the real programming staff sooner. It definitely must have helped because it wasn't too long before I was transferred and became an official "programmer".

As luck would have it, the group I was transferred into had previously employed an experienced programmer who had attempted to write a program that performed the same function as the one that I had written for my former supervisor. The problem was, he never could get it to work right. When my new manager found out I had created a program performing the same function that actually worked, he was very impressed. The major benefit (and unfortunately, eventual drawback) was that he wasn't afraid to throw lots of challenging work my way.

After joining this group, it quickly became apparent who his number one programmer was. She was a very bright person who also produced a large amount of work. It didn't take a genius to figure out who I should approach whenever I had a question about something. Something else I did was go to her for confirmation of concepts or ideas that I had already formulated.

After I had been in the group for about a year or so, she went out on maternity leave. They needed someone to take over the systems she supported. One of them used a database called "DB2". At the time, this was considered fairly new technology. Getting the chance to work on a system like that was an excellent opportunity. I'm still not sure, but I think the manager asked her which person in the group would be the best to take over her work. I believe she recommended me.

This ruffled a few feathers because there were about seven or eight people in the group who would have jumped at the opportunity to work with DB2. In addition, they all had more experience than I did. I think some of them were actually hoping I couldn't handle it. However, I made the most of the break I had been given. I worked exceptionally hard to prove that I deserved the opportunity.

As time went on and I proved myself, I was given more and more responsibility. However, a funny thing happened while I was working so hard...

I looked up one day and discovered that I was supporting about half the systems that this one group had ownership of. On top of that, I'm pretty sure I was the lowest paid employee in the group. I started thinking to myself: "What's wrong with this picture?" In reality, it was a mixed bag, I was receiving valuable experience that eventually led to better jobs and a bigger salary, but there was definitely a price to be paid for it.

Lesson: *Sometimes you get punished for being competent. This was an exceptionally tough lesson to learn. It doesn't seem right, but it's human nature. A manager will give important assignments and more assignments to an employee that can handle it. There is an upside to this, but there can also be a very large downside. The downside is frequently paid for with the hours of your life.*

It got to the point where I was going into work at around 7:00 AM every morning and not getting home until around 8:00 PM at night. It was so bad that I missed my daughter's first steps when she started walking. That was a real wake up call for me.

It all came to a head one afternoon when my manager walked into my office and started questioning me about the pile of Problem Reports sitting on my desk. He wanted to know when they would be completed. I asked him which ones had top priority, so I could focus on those first. He responded with: "They're *all* priority".

I think it must have been the combination of his tone of voice and the fact that I had been killing myself on the job, but my response was simply this:

"Then you need to hire more freaking staff" (I'm a wee bit embarrassed to admit that freaking is a euphemism for the word I actually used...). Amazingly enough, he turned around and scurried out of my office. Fortunately, not too long after this little incident, I was granted a reprieve.

The Chief Information officer (CIO) of the company had created a very small department of Information Technology folks who were independent of the regular programming staff and processes. The entire department consisted of a manager with four people who reported to him.

That manager reported directly to the CIO. The stated goal of the group was to investigate new technologies and determine how they might be applied to the business. Once a promising new technology was identified, a small pilot project might be executed to determine if it was worth bringing into the mainstream IT department. One of the four folks working in that group was transferred into a large reengineering project that was currently underway, which created an opening.

As soon as I heard they were interviewing for that open slot, I applied for the position. Strangely enough, after I interviewed and got the job, I found out that only one other person had applied for the position. I was dumbfounded when I heard this. It was such an obviously exciting opportunity to me that I couldn't understand why more people wouldn't be interested in something like that.

Lesson: *Don't be afraid to take on new challenges and experiences in the workplace. There may be unknowns, but when a real opportunity presents itself, sometimes you have to stick your neck out and go for it.*

When I started this new position, I thought I had died and gone to employee heaven. A recognized part of the job was to read about and research new technology. There were several publications the group subscribed to that were received on a regular basis, then routed around to the four of us. So, it appeared that I had finally found a job where I *could* get paid to drink coffee and read magazines…

One of the new technologies I became interested in was called Object Oriented Programming. Another technology the group had been looking at was called "Expert Systems", which was actually a subset of what is known as "Artificial Intelligence". The goal of an expert system was to capture the knowledge of a human expert into a computer system.

We went on to develop a pilot project that was an attempt to capture an insurance underwriter's knowledge into a system that would be used by Salespeople. A new bonus structure had been put in place that rated a salesperson on the percentage of insurance applications that they brought in which could actually be underwritten. The system we developed would have the salesperson ask certain key questions regarding the existing health status of the applicants. Based on the existing medical conditions, a case would either be accepted or denied. Management figured if this could be determined over the phone it would save time and effort for all involved.

However, right as we were getting ready to pilot test the system, the bonus structure for the sales reps was changed again. The new structure would reward them on the sheer volume of applications they brought in the door, regardless of whether or not they could be underwritten. So effectively, all incentive to use the system went out the door and our project was dead.

At about the same time this project died, a grim financial reality began to raise it's ugly head. I was having trouble paying my bills. By this time, I had received several promotions and held the title of Programmer Analyst. I had also received quite a few raises, but my salary was nowhere near my market value. I learned the unfortunate truth that in many cases, the only way you can really increase your salary is to leave your current employer for another.

I had even gone in and talked to my manager and told him how much I enjoyed my job (which was the truth), but that I couldn't pay my bills. He said he would do some research to determine what someone with my skills and experience should be paid and get back with me.

We spoke again in about a week. He said his research revealed that I was right where I should be, that I was making a fair salary for what I was doing. I asked him where he had gotten his information because my sources and research told quite a different story. He was somewhat vague about answering the question. But the bottom line was: no raise for me.

Immediately after, I began a new job search. In a matter of weeks, I received a job offer for about $6,000 more than I was currently making, plus an annual bonus. I wrote up a letter of resignation and presented it to the same manager. He looked at it, then asked if I would mind telling him how much the offer was for. When I told him, he asked me if I would stay if the company matched the offer. At that point, I was thinking to myself: "What? Why didn't he just offer me the money before? Why did I have to go out and get another job offer before they would cough up the money I was worth? ".

Lesson: *Unfortunately, in many cases, the only way to increase your salary to market value is to change jobs. Even though it doesn't seem like it would be profitable for an employer to lose a valuable employee who has knowledge of the business and bring someone else in and train them, many employers seem to follow the strategy of letting existing employees leave instead of attempting to retain them.*

Fortunately, I was prepared to answer the question because I had done some reading that advised never to accept a counter offer from your company. From that point forward, the company might think you were disloyal. If there were layoffs, your name could be first on the list. So I thanked him, but then explained I had already accepted the job offer and that I did not like to go back on my word.

When All Else Fails, Walk Fast

The interview that I had for my new job was different than any I had ever experienced before or since. I had noted on my resume that I had experience with Object Oriented programming. As it turns out, the Director I interviewed with fancied himself an Object Oriented programming buff. When he saw that my resume listed Object Oriented Programming, he jumped up (and I mean it, he literally jumped out of his chair), went over to the wall of his office and flung open two paneled doors that concealed a large white board. He thrust a marker into my hand and said: "Draw an Object Oriented design on the board".

After my initial surprise, I quickly realized that he was dead serious. Knowing that this was where I would make or break the interview, I figured I would take the initiative and started asking him questions about what he wanted the system to do. At some point, he started grabbing Object Oriented books off of his shelf and thumbed through them, asking me questions.

So there I was, up at the white board, drawing some half assed design for an imaginary system he was making up off the top of his head. All the while he was rifling through an

Object Oriented design book, throwing questions at me about terms and concepts that caught his eye. Fortunately, at some point, he seemed satisfied that I had done enough "designing" and asked me to sit down again.

It seemed I must have passed the impromptu design session because he started talking about an Object Oriented project they would soon be starting. He said that if they hired me, I would be part of the team. A few days later, they made me a formal job offer that I accepted.

After I had been working there a little while, I noticed that this same Director was an incredibly fast walker. He was a short guy, but he could cover some serious ground in a hurry. He was darn near at a dead run whenever he went through the hallways. We used to joke that instead of giving people interviews, he should just take them out to the parking lot and walk them around. If they could keep up with his pace, hire them on the spot.

Unfortunately, I soon found out that things were not quite what I had expected from the interview. The Object Oriented project never quite got off the ground, so I was assigned to doing routine programming tasks with virtually no chance of expanding my skills. Realizing that this was a dead end for me, I resigned myself to putting in the minimum amount of time I would need before I could start interviewing again for another job.

However, before that happened, I had a "one on one" meeting with the same Director (He was the type of upper manager who holds personal meetings with his employees at least once a year). He asked me if I liked what I was doing. I told him no. He asked me if it was challenging. I said no. Then he used a phrase I have never heard anyone actually use before or since: "So, you could do this job while standing on your head, spitting nickels, is that right?" I let out a small laugh and said: "Yeah... probably".

I answered him so honestly for two reasons. I sensed that his questions were motivated by a genuine concern (a rare quality in a manager). The second reason being that I was on my way out the door anyway, so I figured I had nothing to lose. *He* also knew I was on my way out, it was just a matter of time. At the end of the session, he promised that he would try to find something more interesting and asked me to hang in a little while longer.

He was good for his word. About a month later, he called me into his office and asked if I wanted to interview with the company Database Administrator. He needed a part-time assistant because he had so much work on his plate. When I was offered the position, I jumped at the opportunity.

Database Administration was a field that was in great demand. It also had the potential for a much larger salary. I approached it with the same type of fervor I had when I first started programming. I began taking the manuals home to study. I would read them in bed at night before going to sleep. I was determined to become an expert.

Unfortunately, a familiar scenario began to raise it's ugly head. Before long, I discovered that I was putting in a lot of hours at work. It soon became apparent that the Database Administrator (let's call him Ravi) I was working with was perhaps the most driven and demanding individual I had ever met in my entire life. Whatever I did at work never seemed like it was enough. He always wanted more. He had all these grand plans that he wanted to implement and he was limited to a staff of one.

In all fairness, he didn't expect anything out of me that he didn't ask of himself. He put in some incredible hours. In addition to being dedicated, he was also exceptionally bright, one of the most intelligent people I have ever met. As for me, I was willing to put in around 50 hours a week, but that was about as far as I was willing to go. I had a wife and two small daughters. I didn't want to be a stranger to my family because I was never home.

After about six months, the Director, "Mr. Walk Fast", promoted Ravi to a management position. I think he saw a little of himself in Ravi (they were both classic type "A" personalities) and wanted to do anything he could to help further his career.

Tip: *Managers love it when they see what they believe to be their own admirable qualities in an employee. I'm not saying you should change your behavior based on your manager's personality, just be aware that most managers love a "Mini Me".*

When Ravi was promoted to management, I became the full time Database Administrator. While this was a great opportunity, it also meant I had even more work and expectations thrust upon me.

In an effort to reach some type of happy medium, I attempted to develop a rapport with Ravi, but he remained fairly stand offish. He was very reluctant to let his guard down about anything. I also noticed that various books with such frightening titles as "Employee Management" and "Motivating Employees" began to appear on his bookshelf. All I can say is God help the employee whose newly made manager starts buying into all the Management 101 crap.

Now I was afraid that I would have to deal with a manager who was going to try to "motivate" me to achieve more. And that "more" would have to be on top of the 50 hours a week I was already working. I began to feel a familiar sickness in the pit of my stomach...

However, as luck would have it, a young guy at work that I had become good friends with also happened to be one of Ravi's friends. His name was Larry. He and I were discussing the situation one day. I told him that I wasn't sure what to do. No matter what I did, it wasn't enough for this guy, I just couldn't get anywhere with him.

Larry laughed and told me that outside of work, Ravi was a totally different person. He was an incredibly funny, boisterous guy, particularly after he had a few beers in him. The person he described was a "Mr. lampshade on the head, life of the party" kind of guy. I said: "Are we talking about the same person? There's no way this guy is a party animal, he's so serious all the time". He said: "*John*, you have to see it to believe it. Trust me, the guy is a freaking riot". He suggested that I needed to come out after work some time to have a few beers with the guys. He and Ravi were part of a small group who regularly met after work for happy hour.

I had never really been into the "beer buddy" type of thing, but I decided I would go with these guys one night just to see what it was like. Plus, I was very anxious to witness this total personality transmogrification that Larry had described.

I found out that everything Larry had said was true. Not only was Ravi totally hilarious outside of work, he had a dynamic, magnetic personality that had never shone through before. I had so much fun that I went on to become a regular. The group eventually settled with five of us who went out about once or twice a week after work for a few beers.

It was kind of surprising and a little out of character for me to become a regular at happy hour. However, there was one overriding reason: All of these guys were extremely intelligent. Collectively, I can't think of another group of people that had more brainpower or wit. The conversation was always thought provoking, incredibly wide ranging, and funny.

We even developed an acronym for our "meetings". A Ruby Tuesday's restaurant had opened within walking distance from the office. It became our de facto hangout. We began to refer to it as the "First Floor Conference Room" or just FFCR. Occasionally, I would come back from an afternoon meeting to find a post it note on my monitor that simply said "FFCR 5:00". Sometimes Larry and I would walk down to Ravi's office around quitting time and bug him to leave while he was on the phone doing business. We would roll our heads, give him big beer eyes, and point downstairs toward the First Floor Conference room.

Well, all good things must come to and end and so did this. After about two years of experience as a Database Administrator, I found myself in a familiar situation: I was making less money than my market value. I had to leave when I was offered a job making $14,000 more than my current salary.

My Life As a Consultant (Or How I Was Able to Work a 40 Hour Week Again)

My new job was with a consulting firm. It was a somewhat unusual turn of events that led to me accepting a position as a consultant.

I had run into a friend of mine at lunch one day. He and I had worked together on my first programming job, but it had been a few years since I had seen him. He told me he was working as a Database Administrator for a consulting firm on an outsourcing contract. The employer was actually a large IT Services firm that had a multi-year outsourcing deal with a large telecommunications company. They were looking for another Database Administrator, but they wanted that person to be an employee, not a consultant. I interviewed for the job and it went very well, but when the offer package was mailed to my house, the salary was *way* too low.

I called the hiring manager back and told her I had received the offer letter and was very interested in the job, but the salary wasn't sufficient. She asked me what my requirements were. I told her, but she said there was no way they could offer that much. It was a strange conversation, because I could tell by the way she was talking to me that she wanted to hire me and would have given me the money if she could. At the end of the call, she said: "Perhaps I'll see your resume come across my desk again real soon". After I hung up the phone, I realized what she was trying to say.

I contacted the consulting firm that my friend worked for and told them about the situation. They were very interested, so I gave them my resume. A couple of weeks later, I was interviewing for the very same job, but as a consultant instead of as a potential employee. The consulting firm was able to negotiate an hourly rate that provided the kind of salary I was looking for. I never found out the real issue with why the employee salary offer was so low, but I have an idea.

My guess is that they were willing to pay a higher salary to a consultant because the funding for that came from a different place than a fulltime employee salary. I believe there also may have been a misunderstanding about my level of experience when they processed the paperwork for the employee position. Anyway, it all worked out well, because I wound up getting a substantial boost to my salary when I accepted the consulting job.

As a consultant, I was paid by the hour. Any hours I worked over 40 were billed to the client. I received "straight time" for anything over 40, meaning my normal hourly wage, no time and a half. While many blue-collar workers would wince at the idea of no time and a half for anything over 40, that's just the way it is in the IT industry. For some reason, they never pay time and a half for overtime. However, for someone who was used to working on salary (as a salaried employee, you don't get paid for anything over 40), this was a beautiful thing. Not only was I compensated for any overtime, but the client was forced to think twice before having a consultant put in extra hours because it cost them real dollars. Almost magically, I was working a 40 hour week again. It was a beautiful thing.

Not only that, but I discovered that there was a real family type of atmosphere working on this contract. The employer was a large, family oriented company that didn't just give it lip service, they believed it and practiced it. In general, even the employees worked a regular 40-hour week. In addition, most everyone there was friendly and easy to work with.

After working there for a while, I started receiving hints that I should consider "rolling over" and becoming an employee. They weren't allowed to directly solicit me, but they could make the desire known without actually stating it directly. My consulting firm wasn't too happy about it, but they weren't about to say no to a large client that they had placed several of their employees with.

After some preliminary discussions, I realized that I could increase my salary by becoming an employee (for some reason, they were now willing to offer me a salary that was in the range of my market value). In addition, their benefits were excellent, much better than I had with the consulting firm. There were a couple of years left on the contract for the outsourcing deal and the indications were very good that the contract would be extended for additional years. So, when all this was combined (more money, approximately 40 hours a week, better benefits, friendly work environment, apparent stability), it was a difficult offer to resist. I went ahead and became an employee.

During my first year as an employee, I achieved excellent results. I worked very hard and came up with several ways for the Services Company to save money for the client (the telecommunications company). However, much to my surprise, when I received my first formal review, I was rated as an average employee.

This was something new to me, I had never been rated as average in my entire life. When I asked the manager what someone had to do to receive a superior rating, she said something like: "Oh, don't be disappointed about that, very few people get the top rating, it's really kind of an exceptional thing, most people are rated as average." I even asked some of my fellow employees about it and they confirmed the fact that hardly anyone ever received the top rating. They even had a term for it: "Walking on Water".

I didn't dwell on it too much because I was pretty happy with the job, my salary increase was good, and the bonus I received was great. I didn't realize it at the time, but this was actually my first exposure to a quota system or bell curve with regard to employee ratings. Perhaps my previous employers had also used a quota system, but I was totally ignorant to it.

Lesson: *Many employers use a quota system or bell curve to perform employee evaluations. The result is that you're not evaluated against an objective benchmark of performance to determine your yearly evaluation. In actuality, you are rated against the people you work with. If you aren't perceived (notice that I said **perceived**) as being better than your peers, you won't receive an above average evaluation. Sometimes,* *depending on how the bell curve is administered, you may not even receive an average evaluation.*

I continued to work hard the next year (well, maybe not quite as hard, my Momma didn't raise no fool), and my results weren't quite as outstanding as they were the year before but they were very good. I had already run through the entire cost/benefit equation in my head with regard to the chances that I might actually receive a top rating and had come to the conclusion that I could bust my ass the entire year and there might only be a slim or nebulous chance that I would receive a top rating. So, in a case like that, I figured that if you killed yourself chasing the carrot that was always just out of your reach, who was the fool?

So, you can imagine my total surprise when I received my next evaluation. There it was, in black and white, I was now considered a top performer. Not only that, but the manager went on to explain how I warranted the much coveted but rarely seen "Walk on Water" designation. I didn't even have to ask, she expounded on the subject for probably five minutes in glowing tones. This was when I learned that my top rating was due to something I had thought was no big deal, but to management, it was obviously a litmus test that I had passed with glowing colors.

During the preceding year, my manager had asked me to come into the office for an "off the record conversation". The topic was "how can we help a lost sheep back into the fold?".

There was a young woman who had been hired fresh out of college to work on the contract. She had been there for a while, but was floundering badly, she didn't have a clue about what she was doing. However, she was a very pleasant person, and everyone liked her. In addition, at that time, the philosophy within the company was that a person didn't fail. If they weren't succeeding, it was because the system was failing them. Therefore, every effort was made to help an employee be successful.

Accordingly, management had been doing everything they could to help her out. However, all had been for naught, her performance was still sorely lacking. They had one final thing they wanted to try, but it involved a "sacrifice" on my part. They wanted to know (and the question was asked with a great deal of trepidation) if I would be willing to give up my "window cube" (gasp!) for the "cause".

Anyone who has ever worked in an office knows what a big deal office and cubicle assignments can be. For some unknown reason, I had been assigned to a "primo" cube that had a window, which was a big deal to some people. In this case, the reason they wanted me to give up my cube was so the programmer could be located closer to the other people within her group. The rationale being that if she was brought "into the fold" with all the other programmers, they could take her under their wings and help her to "fly", so to speak.

I told the manager that I didn't mind giving up my cube "For the Team". In addition, I was also sworn to secrecy. I couldn't tell anyone why I was being moved out of my window cube because it was such a sensitive situation. I told her I had no problem understanding and accepting that. I was willing to do whatever I could to help the situation. The upshot of the whole thing was that some people thought I was being punished or somehow demoted because I lost my window cube.

Fellow employee: "Hey, what are you doing in this cube? What happened?"

Me: "I don't know, they just asked me if I would move over here, they didn't offer any explanation, and I didn't ask…"

Fellow employee: "Wholly crap…you lost your window cube… man, that's not good. So… it's like you're being punished or something, did you screw up or piss someone off?"

Me: "Not that I know of, it's a total mystery to me"

Fellow employee: "Well, what did they do with your old cube?"

Me: "Blank moved into it".

Fellow employee: "What? What the heck is with **that?** Very strange… well, I hope everything works out OK for you…"

Getting back to my performance review and the unexpected rating: This was perceived as my major "accomplishment" of the year. It was the "differentiating factor" that made me "Walk on Water". It was perceived by my management as the most important thing I did that entire year. It was the deciding factor for why I was now considered an "exceptional" employee.

Lesson: *Sometimes, your performance is evaluated by things that have nothing to do with how well you perform your job. You should always be aware of topics and situations that might be perceived as a litmus test of your* *loyalty or ones that might determine whether or not you'll be recognized as a "Team Player".*

Of course, now that I had finally found a position that I really liked, working in a good environment, making a good salary, it was just a matter of time before things went South…

One day, we were all hurriedly called into a meeting. The general manager announced that the outsourcing contract was not being renewed. The telecommunications company had decided to take all the IT applications that they had outsourced back "in house". He assured everyone that they would have jobs. He said they were actively seeking new business, so no one had to worry about the future. Things looked good and there were plenty of opportunities.

I went home that night and thought about the situation. I had a gut feeling that all the talk about lots of new business contained a lot of spin control, as it later turned out, I was right. In the mean time, I decided not to wait to see if they were able to attract other business. Fortunately, my new employer was a large Multi National Company that actually had another site located in the same town. That location had been around for many years and it seemed like a solid, stable environment. I found out that they had an open requirement for a Database Administrator. I interviewed for and was offered the job. Thankfully, my manager let me transfer into that division of the company.

Look at Me When I'm Talking to You (Or at Least Try to Stay Awake...)

The division I transferred into was engaged in the development and support of various network and connectivity applications. As I said before, they had been around for quite a while and it seemed like a very stable environment. However, almost as soon as I began working there, rumors started flying around that the division was up for sale. Coincidentally, there were also a few upper level managers who moved on to "new challenges", so it seemed that the rumors floating around were probably more than just idle grapevine chatter.

Tip: *When mangers and key players take new positions or move to outside departments, it's usually a tip off that a reorganization or some type of major change may be forthcoming.*

A few months down they road, they announced that a large telecommunications (telco) firm was purchasing our division. Approximately sixty percent of the employees would go to the buying company, the other forty percent would stay. The upshot was that the employees had no say in the matter, we were just pawns in the deal.

I wound up being part of the sixty percent who were "sold" to the telco. We were told that our salaries would remain the same and that the benefits were comparable to what we currently had. There was also a one-year "lock out" for the employees who were sold. Within the first year, our original company was not allowed to hire us back.

A month or so after the switch occurred, my new company sent me a retention letter. They offered a several thousand dollar bonus for me to stay with them for at least a year. I started thinking that maybe this wasn't so bad, they seemed interesting in wanting to retain the employees, so maybe there was a future.

After the buy out was official, I was assigned to a new manager. During one of our first "one on one" meetings in his office, I noticed that his head had begun to… move around oddly… Amazingly enough, he was doing the old "I'm so freaking tired, I'm falling asleep" head bob.

I thought I had seen it all, but I have to admit, this was a new one on me. I'd never yet had a manager who was rude enough or perhaps just bored enough to fall asleep while I was talking to him. I managed to rouse him a little by talking louder, then asked him if he wanted to meet later. He said no, we could keep on going, he was just a little tired because he had gotten back late from a bus trip the night before.

Being friendly, I asked him what type of trip. He said that he'd been to a religious convention. He went on to mention that the most impressive speaker was a man named "Creflo A. Dollar" (no, I'm not making this up… it's the truth, and that's his real name…). A google search revealed this wikipedia entry about Mr. Creflo A. Dollar:

"Many of Dr. Dollar's followers believe that his Rolls Royces, private jet, million-dollar Atlanta home and Manhattan apartment confirm the validity of his "prosperity gospel" teachings. Critics, however, believe his lifestyle is proof of nothing more than the generosity of his parishioners and their faith in God's blessings."

At least it was good to know that my time with my manager was being upstaged by someone who was obviously… "Prosperous" in so many different ways.

After our brief discussion of Dr. Dollar, I continued my status report, which promptly caused my manager to start dozing off again. This pattern went on to repeat itself during approximately one third of our future meetings: Me talking, him dozing. However, there was an upside: I never received any challenging questions while delivering my status report.

Honesty is The Best Policy (And Other Lies)

Even though the telco had bought out my division of the company, they were still sharing the same computer systems with the old company. The contract allowed a certain amount of time for the telco to purchase it's own computer hardware and to migrate the systems and data over, so everything would eventually be totally separate from the old company.

The vast majority of the systems were mainframe applications. However, some genius on the telco side decided that buying or leasing a mainframe was too "expensive", so this led to one of the most bizarre technological decisions I have ever seen.

Another dunderhead came up with the brilliant idea to purchase UNIX servers that could work in parallel and migrate all of the mainframe applications to this platform. In addition, as a "small part" of the effort, they would convert all the databases from DB2 to Oracle. And lest I forget, they had a timeframe of a little over a year to accomplish this.

Now, anyone who knows anything about mainframes, UNIX, and databases will already know that this does not fall into the *"Boy that's a tough assignment, but we'll give it the old college try and make it work"* category.

No, it falls into the *"I can't believe someone could be so breathtakingly ignorant that they would come up with that idea "* category. And on top of that, with a deadline of a little over a year. This was the sort of hair-brained scheme that should evoke a roll on the floor, *"Are you freakin' kidding me?"* type of response from anyone who is even semi-competent.

So, imagine my concern when I wound up having a discussion about this with a high level manager (He was two levels above my manager). Realizing how politically sensitive the situation was, I even tried to be diplomatic about it. The conversation went something like this:

Me: "The timeframe for the project is... fairly aggressive, have you spoken to anyone who has done the same type of effort to get an idea of the issues they faced and how long it took?"

Big Manager: "Why would we want to do that? There are people who run their mission critical applications on UNIX every day".

Me: "That's true, but... those applications were developed from the ground up to run on that type of technology. Taking existing applications that were developed for the mainframe and attempting to move them over to the UNIX platform is a totally different proposition".

Big Manager: "What do you mean?"

Me: "Well, for example, there's JCL (which stands for job control language). We have all of these large batch jobs that are controlled by JCL. You can't just take that JCL and drop it on the UNIX platform and have it run.

Big Manager: "But UNIX has a job scheduler called CRON, can't we use that?". (It would be helpful for the reader to know that JCL and the CRON job scheduler are totally different things, which just points out that this manager was clueless when it came to this entire discussion. It was also my understanding that he was part of the brain trust that had formulated this incredibly wrong-headed idea).

I believe at that point of the conversation, I realized how hopeless the situation was. I had never experienced management that was so blockheaded when it came to technology.

But this is where I made my big mistake. I didn't realize it at the time, but just by voicing concern about this decision, I was now branded as "Not singing out of the same hymnbook" as everyone else.

On all of the other IT jobs I had before, my management expected the IT professionals to play a particular role. Part of that role was to tell the truth and to voice their opinions when it came to technology. It was part of your job and part of your duty. I didn't fully understand it, but I was now working with management that didn't necessarily subscribe to that philosophy. Their philosophy was more along the lines of:

"You're either for us or against us".

A few months after the conversation with Big Manager, I was summoned to my manager's office late in the day (it was after five o'clock). When I came in, he told me to close the door.

I can't even remember what he said, but not too long into his discussion I realized exactly what the meeting was all about. I said to him:

"You're going to lay me off, aren't you?"

He said: "It's not a layoff, it's a *transition*."

Yeah, it was a transition right to the ranks of the unemployed…

Amazingly, he managed to stay awake during the entire conversation….then I got to experience the sublime glory of being escorted back to my office to gather up all my stuff into boxes, then he escorted me out the front door and took possession of my badge. At that point, I was able to practice what I had promised myself after seeing so many people get whacked over the years. I stayed calm and kept myself together, I didn't fall apart. But let me tell you, it's not a pleasant experience any way you look at it.

I'll never know for sure exactly why I was included in that layoff, but I'm pretty confident that my conversation with Big Manager had something to do with it.

After that situation, I promised myself that I would be very careful about giving an honest opinion again unless I knew all of the politics about a situation and had a good feeling that I could trust how it would be received. If not, I would keep my mouth shut.

Lesson: *Be very careful about voicing any politically incorrect opinions at work. Before you open your mouth, make sure you understand the politics of the situation. Even though what you're saying might be the truth, it could be held against you. Even though you might be one hundred percent right, you could wind up being wrong.*

Just in case you're wondering, they never did make the conversion to the UNIX platform. They finally realized that it was an ill-conceived pipe dream.

The Silver Lining

As painful as it was, the dark cloud of my layoff did have a silver lining. About a month after that dark day, I had another job working with my old employer (the one who sold me).

The telco had to pay me my retention bonus (yes, you heard that right, they laid me off, then I received my retention bonus…). In addition, during my first week on the new job, I was still technically on the telco's payroll, so I made more money that first week than I had ever made in my life.

About seven years later, I'm still on the same job. My responsibilities and duties have expanded way beyond database administration. I wear three hats now: Team Lead, Data Architect, and Database Administrator. There was a time when you could specialize in a particular skill, but in today's environment, it makes sense to accept additional roles if they are offered to you. It might help you keep your job.

That brings me to the end of my employment narrative. And to quote the Grateful Dead:

"What a long, strange trip it's been…". And it ain't over
yet…

Life As a Cube Dweller Summary

Tip: *If you ever get laid off (and the chances of that happening are pretty good these days), stay as calm as you can and ask for as much as you can (additional severance, etc). You may not get it, but it certainly doesn't hurt to ask.*

Tip: *If you're ever concerned about being "loyal" to the company, think again. Accept and embrace the reality that you are just a resource to them, nothing less, nothing more. They don't owe you anything. The flip side is that **you** don't owe them anything either. If you have trouble accepting that reality, never forget that if they need to get rid of you, you'll be gone the next day.*

Lesson: *Sometimes you get punished for being competent. This was an exceptionally tough lesson to learn. It doesn't seem right, but it's human nature. A manager will give important assignments and more assignments to an employee that can handle it. There is an upside to this, but there can also be a very large downside. The downside is frequently paid for with the hours of your life.*

Lesson: *Don't be afraid to take on new challenges and experiences in the workplace. There may be unknowns, but* *when a real opportunity presents itself, sometimes you have to stick your neck out and go for it.*

Lesson: *Unfortunately, in many cases, the only way to increase your salary to market value is to change jobs. Even though it doesn't seem like it would be profitable for an employer to lose a valuable employee who has knowledge of the business and bring someone else in and train them, many employers seem to follow the strategy of letting existing employees leave instead of attempting to retain them.*

Tip: *Managers love it when they see what they believe to be their own admirable qualities in an employee. I'm not saying you should change your behavior based on your manager's personality, just be aware that most managers love a "Mini Me".*

Lesson: *Many employers use a quota system or bell curve to perform employee evaluations. The result is that you're not evaluated against an objective benchmark of performance to determine your yearly evaluation. In actuality, you are rated against the people you work with. If you aren't perceived (notice that I said **perceived**) as being better than your peers, you won't receive an above average evaluation. Sometimes, depending on how the bell curve is administered, you may not even receive an average evaluation.*

Lesson: *Sometimes, your performance is evaluated by things that have nothing to do with how well you perform your job. You should always be aware of topics and situations that might be perceived as a litmus test of your loyalty or ones that might determine whether or not you'll be recognized as a "Team Player".*

Tip: *When managers and key players take new positions or move to outside departments, it's usually a tip off that a reorganization or some type of major change may be forthcoming.*

Lesson: *Be very careful about voicing any politically incorrect opinions at work. Before you open your mouth, make sure you understand the politics of the situation. Even though what you're saying might be the truth, it could be held against you. Even though you might be one hundred percent right, you could wind up being wrong.*

PART FOUR

What to do When Your Job Disappears

Surviving a Layoff

If you spend any time at all in a large company or corporation, chances are you will eventually be exposed to the gut wrenching experience of a layoff. Normally, you'll only be an observer, an uneasy witness to the grim spectacle of a group of your fellow employees getting "terminated". However, at some point, you could wind up being part of that unfortunate group.

Here are some of the euphemisms companies use to describe this brutal and potentially life changing event:

Reduction In Force (Or the more commonly used acronym RIF). As in, "Oh, you didn't hear the news? He got RIF'd."

Workforce Reduction

Involuntary Separation

FMP (Forced Management Program)

Job Elimination

Skills Rebalancing (my personal favorite)

No matter what they call it, it all adds up to the same thing. Somebody just lost their regular paycheck. They no longer have a way to put food on the table and pay the bills.

If you ever happen to be on the receiving end of a layoff, there are a few things you can do to help deal with what is potentially a very painful event.

First of all, on the actual day you get laid off, try to stay as cool as you can. Don't be afraid to ask for more severance pay, full payment of all sick time, etc. I know that with large corporations, those issues are usually set in stone, but it doesn't hurt to ask. You have nothing to lose and everything to gain.

If you are immediately taken back to your desk to clean it out, then escorted out of the building, keep your head held high. Try to keep it all together until you get home, then you can fall apart. While we are on the subject of "The day you get laid off", let me give you some advice that was once given to me, but I didn't act on it. Later on, I wished I had.

On any job you have, try to limit the amount of personal possessions you keep at work to a minimum. Before you think I've gone nuts and have totally blown off the subject at hand, consider that each personal item you have to gather up from your office is additional time you will have to spend with your supervisor or the security guard while you load all that stuff into a box. These aren't just idle words on my part either. On the day I got laid off, I was immediately taken back to my office by my supervisor so I could gather up all my junk, then he escorted me out of the building. I had too much stuff to load up, it took way too long to get out of the building, and I should have known better.

I used to work with an old timer who only kept one item in his cubicle: a dictionary, that was it. No pictures, no personal effects, nothing else. One day my curiosity got the best of me and I asked him about it. He said: "I've seen too many people get laid off, then they have to come back to their cube, fumble around, gathering up all their stuff, some of them in tears while they do it. It's way too painful to watch. If I ever get whacked, all I have to do is pick up my dictionary and I'm out the door."

Man, I should have listened to him.

Once you get past the initial shock of it all (and it *is* pretty shocking, no matter how much you think you might be prepared, it still feels like someone knocked the wind out of you), understand that anyone can get laid off. Good employees, fair employees, and lousy employees, it doesn't matter, in today's workforce no one is immune. I mention this because when you get laid off, some very difficult feelings can come to the surface. Probably the most pernicious emotion you can have is a feeling that somehow you did something to deserve it. Even though you may logically realize you did nothing wrong, some strange emotion may bubble up that causes you to feel like you failed in some way.

Where does this feeling come from? It's hard to say, but it may be a vestige of the old Protestant work ethic that still resides in a lot of us. Another factor may be that deep down inside, we still feel that if we work hard and do a good job, nothing bad will happen to us in the workplace. Unfortunately, that is no longer true. You can do an excellent job, be the most dedicated employee in the world, and you can still get laid off.

I had to wrestle with those feelings after I got whacked. Even though logically, I knew I had done a good job and had been a good employee, some of those emotions still floated up to the surface. I knew I had done nothing wrong and there was no blame I should accept for what had happened. However, emotionally, it was a different story.

Another unsettling emotion that might rear it's head is panic. Panic as in:

"Oh my god, I just lost my job, how will I support my family? How will I pay my bills? What if it takes a long time to find another job? What if my skills aren't marketable any more?"

My own personal panic set in when I discovered that there were rumors floating around about the group of employees who were included in the layoff I was part of.

The way that I found out about all this was particularly unsettling. After I was laid off, I approached someone I previously worked with about an opening she had in her department. She was very interested when I told her I was looking for a job. She was obviously excited by the thought of having someone with my skills and experience on her team. I felt pretty confident that I would receive a job offer.

However, after our initial discussion, I suddenly had trouble contacting her. I couldn't get her to return my calls. When I finally made contact with her, she was at least decent enough to tell me what had happened.

When she went to upper management for approval to proceed with the process, they told her of a rumor floating around that the employees who had been laid off were deadwood, sub par performers. She assured them that I was not a lousy employee and vouched for my skills and experience, but her management did not want to take any potential risks. So it died right there, the rumor killed any chance I had of getting that job.

It would be difficult to describe the feeling of despair that swept over me when I hung up the phone. As in many professions, the IT industry is a small world. Your reputation is everything. I was fairly panicked that mine had been irrevocably damaged.

When I applied for my next job, I encountered the same issue. The manager had heard this ugly rumor too. Thankfully, she decided to find out for herself whether it was true or not. She spoke with a few ex coworkers of mine who testified about the quality of my work and my skill level. Another friend of mine was even good enough to go to her office and speak with her face to face. He really went to bat for me and personally vouched for my reputation. Looking back, it would have helped if I had been able to convince myself that the truth would eventually come out about my reputation, but it sure caused me some heartburn in the interim.

Another unfortunate side effect of getting laid off is that your self-confidence can take a hit. This can really set in if it takes a long time to find another position. Try to remember that you're still the same person with all the skills you had before. You held a job for years and were considered a valuable employee, nothing has changed that. You're still as smart and competent as you ever were, you're just a victim of circumstance, plain and simple.

It also helps to stay busy during the period when you're looking for a new position. Approach your job search like it was a regular job. Put a plan together and decide how much time each day you will devote to your search, then do that on a regular basis. It's helpful to have a sense of purpose and to maintain a schedule of some sort.

When I was laid off, I began my new job search the next day. In my case, I was fortunate to be laid off during the early part of 2000, while the tech market was still booming. If you get laid off today, expect that your job search could potentially take a very long time. I've had friends who were out of work a year or more before finding a new job.

Contact your friends and previous office mates. Put the word out that you're looking. It's usually your best bet to find a new job.

If you already exercise on a regular basis, continue to keep your normal routine and maybe even step it up if you can. If you hadn't found time to exercise before because of work requirements, it's an excellent time to begin an exercise routine. Not only will it be good for your physical health, it will also help with your stress level and overall emotional well being.

Stay busy.

Try to remember that this too, shall pass. People get laid off every day and they survive. You will too. Have some faith that you will get through it and may even wind up being better off than you were before

Globalization or "Hey Dude, Where's My Job?"

Globalization… Outsourcing…

We've all heard these terms, but what do they really mean to the average American? Well, if you don't understand them now, once you or one of you friends get to experience the unique pleasure of having to train an overseas job replacement, you'll understand it more than you'll want to.

Remember back in the first couple of years of the new Millennium there was lots of news coverage about the "Jobless Recovery"? The news media posed the question: "Where did all the jobs go?" How could we have a recovery and no new jobs created? They acted like it was all a huge mystery. Well, they had it all wrong. In reality, it wasn't a jobless recovery. If you work in India or China the job market is booming.

The grim reality is this: Many jobs can be performed overseas at a fraction of the cost of an American salary. It typically costs one quarter to one fifth of what it takes to employ someone in America. How can you compete against that? The answer: you don't. Those numbers are just too compelling for companies to not take advantage of them.

So what types of jobs are we talking about here?

My own rule of thumb is this: If you don't need to touch someone to perform your job (Nurse, Physical Therapist, etc.) or if you don't have to work on something that is physically located in the States (air conditioning repairman, power company lineman, etc.), your job can potentially be moved overseas. Sit back for a moment and think about how many jobs fall outside of the "touch someone or something" category.

Pretty frightening isn't it?

The data processing profession has been one of the early adopters of Globalization. Untold numbers of programming, technology, and support jobs are already long gone from this country. Some media pundits have been trying to convince people that Globalization is good for America. They have attempted to make a comparison between the current offshoring of technical jobs and what previously happened to many American manufacturing jobs. The argument is that it will free up American employees to move on to all the "New Jobs" being created, similar to what happened with all the new technology jobs that were created during the 70's and 80's.

Okay... so, I've looked... Where and what are these "New Jobs"? I know I can't find them. Also, even if there were eventually any new jobs created, why wouldn't they be created or moved overseas where the cost of labor is so cheap?

When you examine the simplistic and wrongheaded notion that this is the same thing we experienced in the 70's and

80's with manufacturing jobs, you will quickly come to the conclusion that it's really not the same thing.

Technology has reached the point where an entire segment of jobs do not have to be performed in the States. The technology and infrastructure that makes this possible was not available during the 70's and 80's. In addition, outside of service or medical jobs, I've seen no evidence of new jobs being created that displaced workers can transition into.

So, what type of strategy can be adopted to ensure that your job won't be taking a one-way trip across the ocean? The most obvious strategy is to work in a job that meets the rule of thumb criteria previously mentioned: Make sure you have to touch someone or work on something that's physically located in the United States. Outside of that, it becomes a dicier proposition.

Common opinion used to hold that only repetitive, relatively low level functions would be moved overseas (help desk positions, grunt programming tasks, etc.) There was a false arrogance that real "brainwork" jobs involving Architecture, Design, and Research and Development would stay in the States. However, upon closer examination, it becomes obvious that there is no reason why higher-level tasks can't also be relocated.

Of all the countries in the world, India is uniquely positioned to take advantage of this. The workforce is highly educated, intelligent, and the common language is English. As an example of this, I recently had a discussion with a Help Desk employee in Bangalore, India. To begin with, his English was excellent. Also, during the course of the conversation, he told me he had a Master's Degree in Computer Science. Moreover, he was extremely courteous and said he *loved* his job. It makes you wonder, if the guy on the Help Desk has a Master's degree, what about the folks over there who are doing R&D and Design work? Do they all have PhD's?

So that brings us back to the question at hand. What can you do to protect yourself? How can you make sure you have a job?

If I was younger, I would seriously consider moving into a profession that meets the "touch someone or some thing" criteria. However, I'm not so young anymore and I don't relish having to start all over again. So I'm looking at positions in the technology industry that aren't normally in the first wave of jobs that are exported.

Database Administration, the job I've been performing for the last twelve years has up till now been considered an upper level function that companies don't typically want to outsource. However, that could change in the future. In an attempt to create a margin of safety for myself, I have also assumed "Team Lead" responsibilities. I run low-level team meetings and give project status reports to upper management. Hopefully, this will help to keep my job secure for a little while longer.

It's up to each person to determine whether or not they think they can hang on in their current job path long enough to make it to retirement. I've decided that I will attempt to ride it out as long as I can.

I'm hoping I will make it to retirement without having to flip burgers or say to anyone: "Welcome to CrapMart!".

PART FIVE

Achieving Nirvana (Or How I Learned to Make My Job Not Suck So Much)

It's Just a JOB, Not a "Career"

To those of you who love your career, consider it your "Right Livelihood", and may therefore be tempted to skip this chapter – DON'T. If things ever go South career-wise (and trust me, the Vegas odds aren't in your favor) and you wake up in the middle of the night dreading work the next day, the philosophy laid out in this chapter may serve you like a light at the end of a dark tunnel.

In the introduction to this book, I mentioned that I like to refer to my work as just a job, not a career. You're probably wondering why. In answer to that, let's break out the dictionary and see what it says about the word career. The first two definitions in my dictionary are:

"**1** a general course of action or progress through life. **2** way of living; occupation or profession. "

Now let's look at the definition of the word job:

"**1** a piece of work. **2** a definite piece of work undertaken for a fixed price."

As you can see, there's an interesting difference between the two. One refers to "way of living, general course of action or progress through life." It sounds to me like if you don't love your "career", you might wind up being pretty miserable because it's such a major part of your life.

This career thing almost sounds like something that an executive invented to get more blood, sweat, and tears out of employees: "Let's see… if we call it a *career* instead of a job, they'll think it's more *important,* then they'll work longer hours, maybe even work on weekends… and we won't even have to pay them more! This is pure genius!"

On the other hand, the word job sounds much more limited: "a definite piece of work undertaken for a fixed price."

I know that on the face of it, this may seem very trivial, but this small difference helps you remember and internalize that it's *just a job.* It's a way to put food on the table and pay the bills, not your life's work. That's where the payoff begins for you. Once you start thinking that way, the most amazing thing begins to happen… You start getting some of your life back.

When five o'clock rolls around, instead of toiling extra hours at work, you'll remember that what's not completed today will be there tomorrow. It will also help you to focus on what's really important: going home and having dinner with your family instead of burning the midnight oil at the office.

Don't Forget Who You're Really Working For (And It's Not The Company)

When I started working at the power company, my Father told me: "John, don't ever forget who you're really working for." He went on:

"Your primary interest should be what is best for you, don't ever forget that. You're providing them a service and they're paying you for it, but don't ever forget who you're *really* working for, and that's yourself".

Being only nineteen years old, I didn't fully understand what he was saying. Now, almost thirty years down the road, after having worked for several large corporations, not only do I understand it, I have learned to embrace that philosophy.

It's the only way I've been able to survive.

Just about every company or corporation I've worked for has promoted some type of propaganda that attempts to encourage a feeling of "ownership" among the employees.

Slogans such as: "It's OUR Company" or "We're ALL Stakeholders" are all too common in the workplace. Stop and think about that for a moment.

- Is it really *your* company?
- Do you *really* own a piece of the company?

Most employees don't have a real ownership stake in the company they work for. However, some buy company stock through an employee purchase plan. If you're one of those folks who own a lot of company stock, unless you're getting a big discount on the purchase of it, you might want to reconsider that strategy.

What will happen to you if the company's fortunes take a turn for the worse? If they have a few bad quarters, what does a company typically do? That's right, they lay people off. Nowadays, some companies lay off small numbers of people on a regular basis even when business is good. That type of layoff is so common it's even merited it's own classification: "Stealth Layoff". Because the layoff numbers are small, the event doesn't warrant any press coverage, it flies under the media radar. That's where the "Stealth" part comes in. However, if a company continually does these little layoffs as a matter of routine, over time, it's an effective way for them to quietly get rid of large numbers of employees.

Anyway, let's assume the company you work for begins to experience problems and you get laid off. What has most likely happened to the value of all that company stock you own? There will probably be a little spike in the stock price when the layoffs are announced (investors seem to love layoffs), but in general, the price of the stock will usually be in a downward trend. So, not only are you out of a job, your net worth just took a hit. As you can see, you need to be careful about the "ownership" philosophy.

So why does a company promote the ownership propaganda to it's employees? Sadly, in many cases the real agenda is to take advantage of an employee's good intentions. It's a semi-transparent attempt to leverage their goodwill for the company's benefit. While some of them may actually offer employees real, quantifiable benefits such as large bonuses and stock options that potentially have a big payoff, the vast majority offer hollow statements backed by little or no real monetary benefit for the employee. Unfortunately, even if they get some type of bonus, most salaried employees discover they've been underpaid when they divide the number of overtime hours they work into the bonus amount they receive.

It would be wise for every employee to look at their current job situation with an unbiased eye and ask themselves some questions:

- What is the monetary benefit for all the overtime the company wants me to put in?

- In the long run, how will I benefit from giving my blood, sweat and tears to this company?

- Will my dedication be rewarded in kind?

In the past, many large corporations offered good retirement packages that would provide lifetime security when an employee retired. Even if they didn't offer huge bonuses or stock options, at least the retirement package was a decent tradeoff for the years of dedication and service that an employee gave to the company.

However, in today's world, large corporations are doing everything they can to reduce or eliminate their pension expense liability. Many of them have already converted to "Cash Balance" pensions. The next wave of change is elimination of pensions altogether. Sadly, many corporations have already taken this step.

So, if this is your job situation:

- Little or no retirement benefits
- No stock options
- Little or no bonus
- No real job security

You honestly have to ask yourself why you would be willing to "go the extra mile". Why would you be willing to put in extraordinary amounts of overtime?

Now, a lot of you might be thinking, "Hey, I have to work some overtime to keep my job, this guy is way off base for advocating that I can only put in 40 hours a week " Believe me, I understand that (I'm in the same boat). I realize that most jobs today require some amount of unpaid (or poorly paid) overtime.

What I'm saying is that you need to clearly understand why you're putting in the overtime. If you think it's because you will be generously rewarded for it (either job security wise or money wise), you might be in for a rude awakening. In the vast majority of cases, you aren't really an "Owner" of the company you work for and you won't really benefit from all the additional blood, sweat, and tears you donate to the corporate gods.

One of the benefits of thinking like this is it helps to prevent you from becoming complacent in your job. You'll begin to think more about managing your own career and taking responsibility for your financial future. How many people have made the mistake of thinking "I've been loyal to the company for all these years and I know they'll take care of me". Then a few years down the road, they wind up getting laid off.

Never forget that you need to consider: "What's in this for me?" If you adopt the attitude that you're working for yourself, you'll never forget that you need to put your self interest and welfare first. However, here is the tricky part:

Keep this opinion to yourself. Never, ever, let management think you are operating from your own interests. However, I'm not saying you should lie. What I'm saying is that when you listen to all the company propaganda about ownership, let it go in one ear and out the other, then keep your mouth shut. Don't ever publicly disagree with it. That would be a quick way to commit corporate suicide. Your responsibility goes as far as doing a good job and delivering what your management thinks is important, end of story. You have no obligation to share your thoughts with anyone else, least of all, the company you work for.

Even though companies may publicly state things like "work-life balance", many of them secretly want employees who will put the company's interests before their own. By the same token, do what you need to do for yourself or your family, but don't broadcast it. Your motivations and desires are no one's business but your own.

.

Life Ain't Fair, Get Used to it and Stop Bitching

A major source of frustration and aggravation for many people in the workplace is the concept of "fairness". This is probably because many of us were raised that way. Our parents tell us to treat people fairly, the schools teach us to play fair, popular movies portray that fairness wins out. After a while, it becomes ingrained in our personalities.

However, when we get older and are confronted with unfairness on a daily basis, it can be difficult to deal with. Even though we logically know that life can be unfair, deep down inside, there's still this emotional part of us that yearns for fairness.

If you have any shred of this type of mentality, do yourself a huge favor. At least ten times a day, remind yourself that life ain't fair, particularly in the workplace. It never has been and never will be. I'm not saying that you shouldn't be fair in your dealings with people or that you shouldn't live up to your own code of morality. What I'm saying is don't expect it from other people, and in particular, don't expect it in the workplace.

As an example of this, consider the case where you find out that another employee who performs the same type of work as you makes ten thousand dollars more per year. How would you react to that? Would you feel hurt or betrayed by the company? Would you storm into your boss's office and vent your frustration about how the company isn't fair and how it's taking advantage of you? Or like many people, would you quietly suffer in silence and build up a huge resentment that colors your entire attitude at work?

I think there's another way to look at it. You could consider it a very valuable piece of information that you're glad you discovered. The mentality that allows you to view it that way is because you don't expect life to be fair, *especially* in the workplace.

Once you've gotten past the "fairness" aspect, why should this be considered valuable information? Why on earth should you be glad you discovered it? In answer to that, let's consider the opposite situation for a moment. Let's assume you discover that you're the highest paid person in your position at work. How much room for salary advancement is left for you? When they need to make layoffs at your level, whose salary sticks out like a sore thumb? Don't get me wrong, I'm not saying that you shouldn't go for more money when you get the chance, I'm just saying that you need to consider the up side and the down side of everything.

The reason this is valuable information is because you might have just discovered that you're making less money than your market value. The appropriate course of action is to do some external investigation into the job market to see what type of salary you could command if you moved to another company. You might be pleasantly surprised to discover that you could get a ten to twenty thousand dollar increase just by taking another job.

At this point, instead of going out and securing a job making a lot more money, you might be thinking that what would make more sense is if you went and discussed the situation with your current manager. You're thinking he or she might be able to offer you something close to your market value so you wouldn't have to leave the company. That would make sense, wouldn't it? You wouldn't have to go through the pain and trouble of having to find another job and they wouldn't lose an experienced, valuable employee. Well, I hate to burst your bubble, but it doesn't usually work that way.

Never forget that the company philosophy is to employ you for the least amount of money they think they can get away with. It increases their profit margin, plain and simple. Also, remember that once a company hires you in at a particular salary, the rate of increase is governed by that.

In this case, consider that you're making fifty thousand a year and you discover your coworker is making sixty thousand. That's a twenty percent increase. What do you think the chances are that you'll get a twenty percent increase from the company? When was the last time you received or heard of someone else receiving a twenty percent raise?

Unfortunately, in most cases, the only way you could potentially get that type of increase is if you get another job offer and tender your resignation. At that point, if you're considered valuable, they may offer to match the salary, but at that point, should you accept? It could be risky...

Another fairness issue you will encounter at work is the "fair haired" child syndrome. Just about every manager I have ever known has a favorite employee that gets what seems to be preferential treatment. Instead of getting angry about it, try to figure out why that person gets the special treatment. It could be that your manager puts a lot of stock in someone who has a good "work ethic" (this is typically a euphemism for someone who puts in extra hours) or who volunteers for "special" projects. If you are able to determine that there are particular things your manager likes, unless it goes against your personal values, why not give it to them?

Before you get all worked up about the "extra hours" thing, don't think I'm advocating that you work a lot of extra hours. I'm advocating doing the least amount of extra hours you can while making sure that your manager knows you're putting in those extra hours. If you have a philosophical problem about promoting the amount of overtime you put in, consider this: should the company be asking you to give time out of your life for them? Should your manager expect you to work nights and weekends? Does the company try to get the maximum amount of production out of you for the least amount of investment on their part? You need to start thinking the same way…

If it sounds cold and it sounds hard, well, it is. You know why? Because life ain't fair…

When in Rome (Hey, If They Want to Pay You to do Stupid Things...)

I have to admit, I had a hard time with this concept early on during my working years. If you're a person with a lot of common sense, working in a large company or corporation has the potential to drive you absolutely insane. The amount of stupidity you can encounter is staggering.

So, how does a sane person react when faced with stupidity or when asked to perform a task that doesn't quite make sense? For me, the natural inclination was to try and remedy the situation. I would make recommendations for how to do things quicker and easier. I would sometimes even point out that there were certain processes or procedures that could be eliminated without affecting the outcome or quality of a project. I have even been foolhardy enough to question policies that made no sense to me (a sometimes risky move). The funny thing is that almost without exception, my suggestions and input weren't received with open arms. However, after working in large corporations for a while, I began to understand why this was so.

Reasons Why Stupid Policies/Processes/Procedures proliferate in Companies and Corporations:

- Someone has a vested interest in the stupidity. It could quite possibly be a key part of their job function. Even worse, they may have invented the stupidity.

- The stupidity may have been in existence for so long that it's become institutionalized. In a case like that, you have a snowball's chance of changing it.

- The stupidity may be the result of an executive's decision or mandate. This one is exceptionally dangerous because if you even dare to question it, you could be branded as not being a "team player" or your "loyalty" could be questioned.

- The people you work with are so stupid that they don't understand how stupid the process is.

- The people you work with don't care how stupid the process is and don't want to take the effort to try and change it.

- There may be some double top secret, unknown, political decision behind the stupidity.

Here is a real life example of a policy that I was subjected to in one of my previous jobs. The breadth and scope of the insanity encompassed within this one situation is awe inspiring.

I was working as a Computer Programmer at a magazine publishing company. I hadn't been there very long. In fact, I had just started my first week of "On call" support.

Early one morning while I was asleep, the phone started ringing. While blindly reaching for it, I glanced at the clock. It was 3 AM... Production support was on the other end calling about a problem with a program that had failed. I wrote down the information and told them I would sign on to the system to take a look at what the problem was.

After I signed on, I pulled up the documentation for the program. It read: "Cold program, do not call the programmer at night, contact during normal business hours" (Every production program had a designated "temperature": Cold, Medium, or Hot). The temperature indicated how critical the program was.

I called production support back to relay this information to them. The guy on the other end of the line said: "We don't have any cold programs". As politely as I could after being woken up at 3:00 am in the morning, I asked him to review the documentation because it specifically stated "Cold program, do not call the programmer at night". He said: "I know it *says* that, but we don't have any cold programs, we always contact the programmer..."

Faced with this sort of response, I became a wee bit testy. At that point, I asked to speak to his supervisor. When the supervisor got on the phone, he basically gave me the same answer. I realized I was fighting a losing battle, so I said I would investigate the error and tell them what the solution was later.

When I got to work the next day, I approached my manager to discuss the situation. A funny sort of look came over his face, then he told me: "Yeah, they always call us for every program, it doesn't matter what it says in the documentation." He paused for a second, then added: "But you know… it's your business about how quickly you respond to the problem, do you know what I mean? In other words, ya gotta do what ya gotta do."

Later on that same day, I asked one of the veteran programmers about this. His response was a bit more direct than my manager's response was: "If anyone gets called on a cold program, they just say they're working on it, then they go back to sleep. Everyone does it… but you didn't hear that from me…" I walked away from this with a realization that it was definitely a "Don't ask, don't tell" kind of situation. Everyone knew what the deal was, but no one really wanted to talk about it.

As time went by, whenever my turn in the weekly on call rotation came up, at least once during the week, I would get woken up in the middle of the night for some unimportant program. At first, it was a little hard to do because of that old work ethic thing, but as soon as I found out it was a cold job, I would tell them I was working on it, hang up the phone and try to go back to sleep. Sometimes, I was able to go back to sleep, other times not. I tried not to let it bother me too much, but the more I thought about it, the more angry I would get because I really hate getting woken up in the middle of the night for no good reason.

Once a year, the Director of all the programmers would have an "all hands" meeting. Toward the end of the meeting, he would entertain questions from the employees. I must have been recently subjected to one of those "wake up" phone calls, because I summoned up all my intestinal fortitude and decided to inquire about the mysterious "Don't ask, don't tell" policy.

To say the least, I could tell by the look on his face that I had touched a raw nerve. He said he wasn't aware that the policy was a problem. Then he threw the question out to all the other programmers and managers in the room:

"Is this really that big of an issue? Does it happen often enough to be a problem?"

The response was dead silence.

Then he turned toward one of the managers and asked him if he thought it was a problem. With a deer in the headlights look, the manager responded with something like: "No, not really…". The director turned back to me with a shrug of the shoulders, non verbally communicating that it looked like there wasn't any problem at all, maybe it was just me. After seeing how obvious it was that everyone in the room was too scared to tell the truth, I threw up my hands and said: "Hey, if no one else has a problem with it, I guess it's not a problem to me…"

After that meeting, one of the old timers took me aside and finally gave me the whole story (too bad someone else hadn't told me this before…).

As strange as it may seem, at one time, production support used to follow the directions in the program documentation. If it was a cold job, they didn't wake programmers up in the middle of the night. It seems this system worked just fine until one night when there was a hot, critical program that failed and for some reason, the production support person neglected to call the programmer.

Well, the next day, all hell broke loose when management got pulled in to the situation. It got so bad that it went up the chain all the way to the director level. Eventually, the director of production support wound up in a "meeting" with the director of programming and it turned into a power struggle.

The stance the Production Support Manager took was to defend his staff's incompetence. He declared that it was too potentially error prone to have some programs that the programmer would get called about and others that they shouldn't get called on. He said something to the effect that any program that was in the production schedule should be considered important enough to merit a phone call to the on call programmer at any time of day. If it wasn't important, it shouldn't be in the schedule.

It wasn't clear what exactly happened that caused the Director of programming to fold in this situation (perhaps the production director had some pictures of him in a compromising position, who knows?). But for some unknown reason, he rolled over and agreed to let them wake up the programmers in the middle of the night for non critical jobs that failed.

The same programmer who told me this story had also developed his own method for dealing with the inequity of the situation. He said to me: "Hey, that's all right, whenever they cause me to lose an hour of sleep for no reason, I just make sure I pay them back for twice the amount of time." I was duly impressed, not only was this man a wealth of information, he was a philosopher to boot.

He became my hero.

Faced with these types of situations, in almost all cases, your best bet is to just go with the flow. If you question a stupid policy or try to improve a stupid procedure, you usually only wind up wasting your time and getting frustrated.

On the other hand, you can adopt a philosophy that says: "Hey, if they want to pay me good money to do stupid things and to put up with idiotic rules, I'll take that all the way to the bank".

The Most Dangerous Game

Have you ever noticed how many management slogans use sports based jargon?

- "Let's build a Winning Team"

- "Beat The Competition"

- "Let's Win in the Marketplace"

In Jack Welch's book "Straight From The Gut" he even refers to employees as "A, B, and C players". Oh, Oh, guess you don't want to get slapped with the dreaded "C" player rating do you? (For more on this subject, refer to the chapter in this book entitled "Differentiation or Rank and Yank").

If you understand and internalize that your job is very much a game, it will help you develop a mindset that will allow you to observe the game, learn the rules, and recognize the key players.

Once you begin to recognize the players that management perceives as "Stars" (one of my previous managers actually referred to one of her employees as the "Michael Jordan" of the team), pay close attention to how they speak and act, sort of like you would if you encountered an alien life form from another planet, because, basically, that's what most of them are.

Once in a Blue Moon, the Star Player may actually warrant this designation based on objective criteria with regard to their job knowledge and ability to deliver quality work. However, this is dependent on management possessing the wherewithal to correctly recognize and evaluate these traits. In today's workplace, this occurs with relatively the same frequency as an Elvis sighting. So, more often than not, the Star player has achieved this status by evidencing some traits other than subject matter knowledge or the ability to deliver quality work.

So, what could these other traits possibly be?

Perhaps the most common is an ability to spew bullshit with authority and confidence about subjects for which they have little or no knowledge. The second most common is the talent to provide management with whatever answer (right or wrong, it doesn't really matter) they are looking for. However, this requires the much coveted ability to translate "Management Speak " on the fly.

For example, when someone is asked a question such as: "Can you deliver project XYZ by the end of the first quarter?" or "Can ABC technology be seamlessly applied in our current environment? ", any answer other than a boldly stated:

"Yes, we can deliver! or **"Sure, no problem at all"** has the potential to be negatively viewed.

If you should happen to erroneously respond by intelligently discussing the real issues and tradeoffs that might be involved with attempting to deliver a project by an insanely aggressive date or discuss the real limitations of applying the ABC technology in your environment, you run the risk of being viewed as indecisive or even worse, obstructionist.

This is because, in most cases, when management asks, *"Can you deliver project XYZ by the end of the first quarter?"*, a question isn't really being asked. Indeed, the corporate superstar's semi-reptilian brain automatically understands this and effortlessly morphs the question into something that sounds like: *We've decided to deliver by end of first quarter, are you on board?"*.

 Failure on your part to immediately perform this translation is hazardous to your corporate health. Understanding the rules of the game will allow you to correctly translate this Management Speak.

But why does management ask questions like this instead of just stating that the project has to be delivered by the end of the first quarter? Well, that's where the really slimy part begins.

You see, management is quoting directly from page 69 of the Management 101 manual. They are attempting to elicit *"buy in"* or *"commitment"* from their employees. Management philosophy states that if employees have personally *"bought in"* or feel like they have input into the decision making process they will have more of a personal commitment to deliver on time. However, if the employee already puts in fifty or more hours a week (which seems to be fairly average these days) and is also a hard worker, then what exactly does "buy in" or "commitment" mean? It doesn't take a rocket scientist to figure out that they might actually be code phrases for "work nights and weekends if that's what it takes".

Once you begin to understand some of the language and the rules of the game, what can you do to protect yourself from having to work extraordinary amounts of overtime?

To begin with, at the beginning of a project, when you're asked to give an estimate for how long it will take to deliver something or how much effort is required to perform a task, make sure you've added some amount of padding into your estimate. This, of course is dependent on the other folks you work with. If they perform similar work and also pad their numbers on a regular basis, you're in pretty good shape.

However, if you have one or two people who either out of ignorance or an attempt to suck up to management continually turn in bare bones estimates, after a while, it will begin to force your hand. You won't be able to pad as much.

Estimate padding will protect you from three main things that invariably occur on a project:

- Unforeseen problems
- Poorly defined and constantly changing requirements
- The dreaded "Can you deliver by the end of first quarter?" question.

If you've already added a fudge factor into your estimates, it makes it much easier to handle those types of issues without having to resort to working long nights and weekends.

Something else you should do is sharpen your powers of observation. Once you've figured out who the "Superstars" are, watch what they do and say and how management responds to them. This will provide you with a wealth of information about what your management really values. It will help you determine how the game is actually being played. Each company and department are unique and have their own variations on the rules and how they are interpreted.

Remember, if you fail to figure out these rules, you do so at your own risk.

Differentiation or "Rank and Yank"

If you've never heard the term "differentiation", get ready to pucker up and hold on tight, because it's a pretty safe bet that you probably will at some time in the future.

In a nutshell, "differentiation" is a forced ranking system. The cornerstone of the philosophy is that you should lavishly reward the top twenty percent of employees, let the middle seventy percent continue to work at the company, and drive off the bottom ten percent. The rankings are typically something like A, B, and C, or 1, 2, and 3. The percentages can vary, but the real killer is that you *must* have the bottom percentage.

Every year, the company will designate that roughly ten percent of their employees are underachievers and should seek employment elsewhere. This philosophy was developed, practiced, and preached by Jack Welch, the former CEO of GE. In the early eighties, he was lovely referred to as "Neutron Jack", due to the massive amount of employees he laid off during that time frame. The "Neutron

Jack" moniker is an analogy to the neutron bomb: He wiped out the employees and left the buildings standing.

Since retiring, he has written a book called "Winning" in which he describes and defends the differentiation philosophy. Amusingly, within GE itself, the employees have another name for differentiation, they refer to it as "Rank and Yank".

Interestingly enough, Welch claims that he didn't invent differentiation, he "learned it on the playground." This is a reference to the all too familiar process of choosing captains, then the captains choose their players. The end result always being that the last couple of kids left standing there get to feel like crap. You really have to love that type of "executive" analogy. Not only is it an oversimplification of "differentiation", it's really quite a dissimilar process.

When viewed at a macro level, it might actually be feasible to say: "Hey, we probably have ten percent deadwood within the company that we can get rid of." I don't think anyone with any sense is going to argue that just about every company sooner or later accumulates people that are genuinely low performers. I also don't think that the average person would have huge issues with laying off or even firing the lousy employees. However, differentiation is something quite different.

The philosophy underlying differentiation is not one of identifying people who shouldn't be at the company because they are lousy employees, it is a philosophy that on it's face states that every year, year after year, you must designate ten percent of the company's employees as undesirable and attempt to run them off.

Another potential flaw has to do with the level at which the ten percent gets administered. In some companies, it actually comes down to the lowest level manager. Here is an example: Let's assume that a manager has a department of ten people. That manager is given an allotment of ratings to give out: Two A's, seven B's, and one C. What does the manager do if he or she has no poorly performing employees? You guessed it, they have to give a bad rating to some poor schmuck who did not actually deserve it. In addition, within the middle seventy percent, a morale issue will begin to build and it will fester over time. Within that group there are typically very high performers who get saddled with what is basically a mediocre performance rating and a mediocre raise (at best). The quota system will not allow their manager to give them an above average rating and raise.

While there may be the occasional person who is foolhardy enough to make a Herculean effort the next year in an attempt to achieve the coveted A rating, there are many more who will realize that it's just a shell game and will adjust their work ethic accordingly.

While the company propaganda will typically make some grandiose statement about differentiation being used to foster a "High Performance Culture" or to "Reward Excellence", when you look under the covers, it's quite possible that the real objective of the system might be something else.

In reality, it normally inspires fear and resentment within employees. While fear can be a motivator, I'm not sure if it's one that leads to a "High Performance Culture". It's also a philosophy that has great potential to breed back stabbing behavior between employees because, when it really comes down to it, they aren't being rated on their relative merits against some objective criteria, they are rated *against each other*. So much for team building and cooperation.

I also believe that differentiation is an effort to legitimize constant turnover within a company. But why would a company want constant turnover? Isn't that non-productive? Doesn't it cost a company money? Well... maybe not.

Every year an employee survives at a company, their salary gets bigger and they become more expensive. And while they would never admit it, many companies would love to get rid of the older, more highly paid employees and replace them with younger, inexpensive labor. However, there's this little problem about practicing age discrimination...

So, what's a company to do?

Consider this: as an employee survives year after year in a system that practices differentiation, it gets harder and harder to maintain an acceptable performance rating. Every year, the ante gets increased. Every year they have to prove themselves more. A system like differentiation allows a company to designate a certain percentage of the employee population as underachievers (even if they aren't...) so they can get rid of them. In case you're thinking that they might only be targeting the older employees, which would still constitute age discrimination, rest assured that the smart companies make sure all age demographics are represented in the bottom portion. However, the net result is that it still allows them to get rid of older employees without triggering potential age discrimination lawsuits...

So what can an employee do to help increase their odds of survival in a system like this? That's the $64,000 dollar question.

The most important thing is being able to determine what your management thinks denotes "excellent performance". Take note of the subtle difference between "excellent performance" and "what your management thinks denotes excellent performance". In addition, you also have to find out what types of activities your management thinks are indications of "above and beyond" behavior from an employee. In other words, what are the determining factors when managers rate employees against each other. Make no mistake about it, that's exactly what happens within a system that practices differentiation.

Each company has their own criteria for performance, but here are some that are commonly used:

- Volunteering for "Special Projects"

- Assuming "Additional responsibility"

- Hours worked, or in some cases, hours logged

These are some of the top activities that management frequently looks for when they perform the "Rank and Yank" function. However, the problem with taking on "Special assignments" and "Additional Responsibilities" is that you still have your normal job duties to perform, that's a given. So how do you take on the additional stuff without killing yourself by working seventy hours a week?

One method is to do the minimum required to meet the responsibilities of your normal day-to-day tasks. Bear in mind, I'm not advocating that you shouldn't do your job, I'm saying you should eliminate anything that's not critical and do only what it takes to keep the bear off of your back with regard to your mundane job functions. Also, you need to make sure that the things you no longer do or only meet the minimum requirement for are things your management doesn't measure or think is important (that's key, if management thinks it's important, it's important to you). You also need to make sure you aren't neglecting things that will come back and cause you a problem in the future.

So, if they don't meet any of these criteria:

Does management measure it or think it's important?

Will it cause you a problem in the future?

Consider dropping it like a stone. If you don't start practicing this type of mental "weeding out" at work, while trying to take on all the extra responsibility that will ensure you don't get relegated to the bottom percentage at evaluation time, you'll wind up working so much overtime you'll never see your own life or family again.

If you have any attacks of conscience about not doing your normal tasks to the utmost of your ability, you have to remember what you'll actually get evaluated on and rewarded for. The company made the decision about what was important when they put a rating system like differentiation in place, you'll just be giving them what they asked for.

When You Walk Out The Door at Five, Leave it Behind

Do you have trouble leaving your job behind when you walk out of the office at the end of the day? Do you lie awake at night thinking about the big project you've been working on or the imminent deadline you're facing? Have you ever been guilty of not being fully engaged in conversations with your family because in the back of your mind, you're thinking about some work issue that's bothering you? I guess if your job is truly the most important thing in your life, maybe that makes sense. However, if it's not, you need to stop and think about why you're doing it and what you can do to stop. Do you think that going around in a semi zombie state is fair to your family? In addition, you're probably not doing your employer any real favors either because if you live, eat, and sleep your job twenty four hours a day, it can lead to premature job burnout.

First of all, you need to ask yourself what you're accomplishing by thinking and worrying about the job while you're not there. Do you really think it helps to make the situation better? If the answer is no, it sounds like you need to come up with a different strategy. I understand this because, in the past, I would occasionally take my work home with me. However, for at least the past few years, when the workday is over, I leave it totally behind. When I shut down my computer at the end of the day, the portion of my brain that I devote to work gets turned off too. It wasn't always that way. In the past, even though I might not have been consciously thinking about it, "work thoughts" would occasionally be churning in the back of my mind when I was supposed to be fully engaged in doing something else, like living my own life. However, over time, I eventually got to the point where I could turn it off like a light switch. There are certain methods I used to help get there.

The first of these is the most obvious, but in reality, probably the most difficult to act on. However, with practice and repetition, it can become almost second nature. Whenever the dreaded "Work thought" comes into your head, consciously force it out of your mind. Mentally switch gears and think about something else you're interested in. Pick up a book and read it, go talk to your spouse or one of your kids. Do *anything* other than think about work. It probably won't happen over night, it may take time to get into the habit, but remember the payoff: You'll be getting some of your own time back. You'll be more fully engaged in life. *Do not* allow yourself to think work thoughts away from the workplace.

Here's something else that helped me. It was probably the easiest one to act on and the most effective. Not to be overly morose or dramatic, but have you ever thought about your own mortality?

I mean, *really* thought about it?

I'm 49 years old now. When I "do the math", it's a pretty safe bet that I've already burned through more than half of the years I'm going to get in this life. And just to make things worse, I need to subtract all the working days I'm going to have to put in before I can retire. When I look at it like that, it's really not that hard to convince myself that I shouldn't devote any more time or thought to my job than I absolutely have to.

Something else began to happen after I turned forty that had a huge impact on me.

Some of my co-workers suddenly died. One situation in particular stands out.

Like myself, he was a Database Administrator. I actually spoke with him on the day he died. It was just like any other work day, we had a conversation about the IT profession and how difficult it had become in the past few years. He confided in me that he had recently signed up to take classes in automotive repair. He had decided to chuck the office job and become a car mechanic. I came in to work the next day and found out that he had died later that night. I was never able to find out all the details, but I heard that it was asthma related. The guy was about ten years younger than me.

He spent his last day on earth working at a job he didn't like.

His death made quite an impact on me. For years, I had been rethinking my entire philosophy concerning my relationship to the workplace and how much of my life I was willing to give to the job. That singular event brought it all to a head. I would never look at my job the same way again.

On the positive side, there's a couple of things you may discover once you get into the mode where you're actually able to leave it all behind when you're away from work. You might find that you're less stressed (both at home and work). Come Monday, it might not be such a chore dragging yourself into the office. You may also realize that you're able to focus better at work. You'll come in each day with a better outlook because you'll discover you've gotten some of your life back.

It's made a huge change in the quality of my life. You might find that it has a profound effect on your life too.

Do You Work For NASA? Are You a Brain Surgeon?

How truly important is your job?

- If you screw up, is someone going to die?

- If you lose a moment's concentration, will someone be paralyzed for life?

- If you make an error in judgment, will the rocket blow up?

If you can't answer yes to the above questions, then you'll have to begrudgingly admit that, well… yeah, maybe your job is not really a matter of life and death.

I'm not bringing this up in an attempt to trivialize what someone does to make a living. I'm mentioning it so you can keep the proper perspective on things. Sometimes, it's easy to lose sight of the relative importance of your job in relation to other portions of your life.

Management will attempt to foster the notion that your job is all-important. They want you to give 110% to everything you do. Of course they do… That way, they get more work out of you. If you've convinced yourself that your job is *"Very Important"*, you'll be much more inclined to work weekends or stay late at the office, making sure that the "critical" thing you're working on gets finished.

However, when you stay late or work weekends (particularly if you're on salary), who benefits from that? You or the company? You might have heard the old saying that no one on their deathbed looks back and thinks: "Boy, I wished I'd spent more time at the office and less time with my family". Well, that's one of those tired little pearls of wisdom that happens to be true.

Another side of the "My job is very important" attitude is that, if you're not careful, it can cause you to become a corporate clone. If you wake up one day and discover that you've become the defender of the "Company Line", if you're the guy during meetings who's constantly reminding everyone about the correct procedures and processes to follow, you may need to lighten up and get a life.

Look for the humor in your job. Make fun of the stupidity that you have to deal with on a regular basis. You'll be much happier at work. You'll be a lot more fun to work with too. You might actually discover that you're more productive and effective.

And strangely enough, you may find out that you've got a life outside your job.

Find Your Passion Outside of Your Job

If your job isn't your passion, you should have something outside of your job that you love to do. A key component of the philosophy advocated in this book is that you need to have a life beyond your job. In fact, you want to maximize your "real life" as much as possible. If you clearly understand that your job is just a way to make a buck, it will allow you to devote the minimum amount of your energy to your job and the maximum amount of energy to your real life.

Conversely, if you don't have something outside of work that you are passionate about and you spend an inordinate amount of time working at a job you don't care about or that you hate, that's a recipe for disaster.

If you don't know what your passion is, there are many self-help books that have methods for helping someone to determine what their life's work or passion might be.

One thing that many of them mention is to try and remember what you enjoyed doing as a child. Quite frequently, as we get older, we discard some of the dreams we once had as being irresponsible or unachievable. If you're not sure what your passion is, it might be time to revisit some of those old dreams. You might find that what turned you on as a young person still turns you on today.

Make a list of the things you would like to do or accomplish in your life. There's something powerful about writing your dreams and goals down. It helps you to visualize the things you want. When you visualize what you want, it can become buried in your subconscious mind and feed your imagination. When I did this exercise, one of the things on my list was to write a book. About a year after I made the list, I had a dream about writing one. When I woke up in the morning, I had already written some of it in my head. I immediately sat down at the computer and started to write. About eight months later, I was holding my first self-published book in my hands. Along the way, I discovered that writing and publishing books is something I really enjoy doing and will probably continue to do after I quit or retire from my "real job".

If your passion is some sort of enterprise or business venture, remember that making money is not the primary goal. You already have a day job that pays the bills, you want to follow your passion for the love of it, not the money. If you do wind up making money at it, that's great, but remember that it's not your primary reason for doing it..

Bear in mind that you don't have to quit your job to start pursuing your passion. Sure, it would be great to tell your employer to "Take this job and shove it" and start your own business in pursuit of your dream, but how many people are really in that sort of financial position? Not only would it require a certain amount of money to finance a new business, you would need to have enough money to support yourself until the business begins to turn enough profit to live on. If you are in a position to do that, hey, that's great, go for it and don't look back. However, there is an alternative. You can start investigating new passions and ventures while you keep your current job.

If you're sitting there thinking there's no way that will happen because you have to devote so much time and effort to your current wage slave existence, you need to do some serious evaluation about where you're at and what your future looks like.

If you're working in a job that you don't like and it consumes so much of your time and effort that you can't even begin to start pursuing something else, where does that leave you? If nothing changes, where will you be in five years? If you want things to get better, it will require a willingness on your part to change your mindset about your current job and start making some changes.

A good place to start is to consider how much time and effort could potentially be eliminated from your job while still remaining employed. Can you apply a seventy or eighty percent effort to your work instead of one hundred percent? Are there any tasks you normally perform that can be totally eliminated? If you seriously consider what could be reduced or not done at all, you might be surprised. Is there any potential risk in adopting a strategy like this? Of course there is, but if you make sure you're still delivering what your management thinks are the most important things, it goes a long way toward mitigating that risk.

If you review your job situation and come to the conclusion that there's no way you can reduce your time or effort, you need to make sure you're really taking a cold, hard, logical view of the situation. Make sure you're not hidebound by preconceived notions about what your "duty" is or what you "ought" to do. After taking this second, unemotional view of your situation, you're still convinced there is no way to reduce your current effort, you need to consider looking for another job that won't require as much of your time.

A funny thing happened when I adopted this new approach to my job. When I focused on delivering the things my management thinks are important and stopped doing things I thought didn't have to be done, my job didn't suck quite as much, it actually got better. My management also seems to be very happy with my performance. In addition, I now have some time to do what I really want to do with my life.

And let me tell you, that's a great feeling.

Afterword: It's Not Cynicism, It's Reality

After I finished writing "My Job Sucks", I sat down and read it from cover to cover.

I realized that someone who has not worked in corporations or large companies for an extended period of time might think my perspective was overly cynical. On the other hand, I'm sure that anyone who has worked in those potentially soul-sucking environments will recognize and relate to some of the situations in this book.

If any of the examples I've presented seem extreme or unfair, rest assured that it wasn't through exaggeration or distortion of reality on my part. The way they are described is the way they really happened. Accordingly, I knew that I would run the risk of this book potentially having what some readers might consider to be a negative tone. However, I made a conscious decision to not gloss over facts and events. I wanted to produce a book that honestly presented the reality of today's workplace.

Sure, there are some people who maintain a naïve attitude and refuse to accept reality. They want to believe that their employer is all warm and fuzzy and paternalistic. However, there are very few companies or corporations left today that still adhere to those standards. Moreover, that type of expectation on the employee's part has the potential to cause a great deal of heartache and disappointment. Unfortunately, those who maintain that kind of expectation may wake up one day and find that they are forced to face the cold reality of the modern work environment. Events such as layoffs, unfair performance appraisals, and outsourcing of jobs don't just happen to "other people", they can happen to anyone.

On the bright side, once you recognize and accept the fact that the workplace has it's own bizarre rules that quite frequently fly in the face of fairness or common sense, you can develop strategies to protect yourself and survive.

And yes, with the right mind-set, you can even thrive in the corporate environment.

That's what this book has been all about.

Resources

Books:

Corporate Confidential : 50 Secrets Your Company Doesn't Want You to Know --- and What to do About Them

Author: Cynthia Shapiro
Publisher: St. Martin's Griffin
ISBN: 0312337361

Do you ever get the feeling that your company says one thing, but actually does something else? This book, written by a former Human Resources Executive verifies that in many cases, your feeling is justified. It also goes on to explain why companies quite frequently say one thing and do another.

I recommend this book with a caveat. I enjoyed the first sections more than the later parts. While the advice in the later sections might actually help you promote yourself and your career, you would have to be able to stomach becoming a corporate clone and yes man/woman. However, it's well worth the read because it provides an accurate view into the mind-set of Corporations and their Human Resources policies.

A Working Stiff's Manifesto: A Memoir of Thirty Jobs I Quit, Nine That Fired Me, and Three I Can't Remember

Author: Iain Levison
Publisher: Random House Trade Paperbacks
ISBN: 0812967941

Not only is this book well written, it's totally hilarious. Having worked in several blue collar jobs, I can testify that it has the ring of truth to it. I absolutely love the part about working in the stainless steel room on the fishing ship with the "Panic Button".

An excellent read that is wickedly funny.

Index

Order Form

Fax Orders: 813-907-2652. Send this form.

Toll Free Telephone Orders: 866-362-0599

Email Orders: everlovebohannon@aol.com

Postal Orders: Everlove and Bohannon Publishing, PO Box 7411 Wesley Chapel FL   33544-0107

I want ____ copies of **My Job SUCKS and I Can't Take it Anymore! HELP!** For $18.95 each.

Name:_____

Address:_____

City/State/Zip:_____

Telephone:_____

Email:_____

Sales Tax: Please add 6% for books shipped to Florida addresses.

Shipping: $4.00 for the first book and $2.00 for each additional book.

My check or money order for $_____ is enclosed.